ENDORSEMENT

"Tim Chambers is a fellow artist who creates beautiful paintings, not in spite of—but because of—his weakness. His personal story and amazing works of art show us all how to lay before our great Creator our own limitations, for only in doing so can the Master Artist have his way with his brushstrokes across our lives. Tim's inspiring story will touch your heart!"

JONI EARECKSON TADA
Joni and Friends International Disability Center

"I know and respect Tim Chambers. I deeply appreciate his artistic gifts and skills, his desire to honor God, and how he has faced significant adversity. I commend Tim as an artist and a person."

RANDY ALCORN
Author of *Heaven*, *If God Is Good*, and *Happiness*

"Tim Chambers and his incredible talents have been a part of Prison Fellowship since he painted the masterful portrait of our founder, the late Charles Colson. That portrait still hangs in the main corridor of the Prison Fellowship Guest House—greeting hundreds of visitors to our complex each year. Despite Tim's physical limitations, he continues to use his talents to glorify God and expand His kingdom. His latest creation is this magnificent adult coloring book, which will bring hope to our incarcerated men and women. As the Lord told us to 'remember those in prison,' we celebrate Tim's latest creation which will minister directly to each one of them."

JAMES ACKERMAN
President and CEO, Prison Fellowship

"There is no adult coloring book I can recommend more than my good friend Tim Chambers' *Seeing Beautiful*! It's the perfect combination of coloring yourself happy and feeding your soul with beauty!"

TRACY KLICKA MACKILLOP
Director of Development, Homeschool Foundation

SEEING BEAUTIFUL
through the journey of life

A COLORING BOOK TO
SEE WHAT YOU'VE BEEN MISSING

TIMOTHY J. CHAMBERS

BroadStreet
PUBLISHING

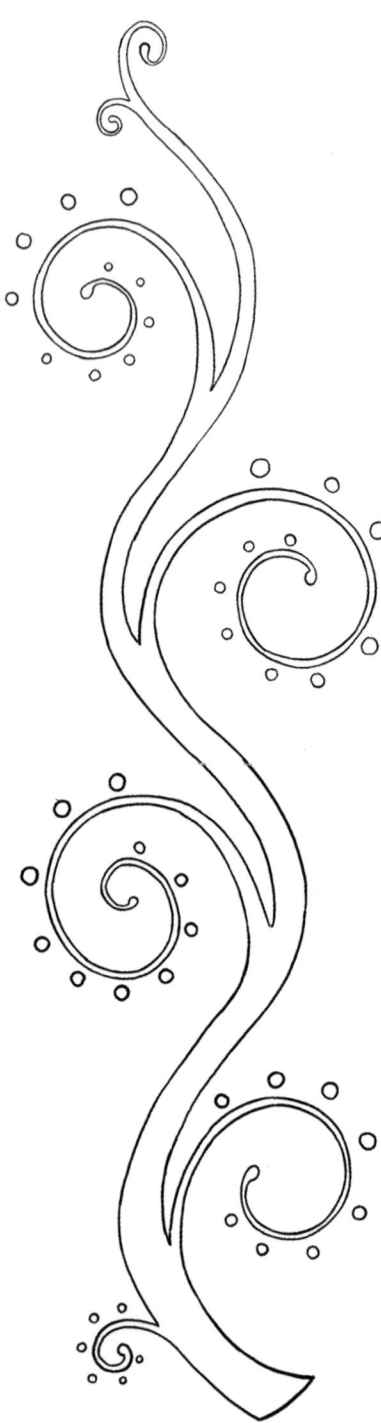

BroadStreet Publishing Group, LLC
Racine, Wisconsin USA
BroadStreetPublishing.com

Seeing Beautiful

ISBN 978-1-4245-5463-8

Copyright @ 2017 Timothy J. Chambers
in association with 17° Creative Group, 17creativegroup.com

All rights reserved. No part of this publication may be reproduced, distributed, transmitted in any form, by any means, including photocopying, recording, or other electronic or mechanical methods, without the prior written permission of the publisher, except in the case of brief quotations embodied in critical reviews and certain other noncommercial uses permitted by copyright law.

Scripture quotations marked NLT are from the Holy Bible, New Living Translation, copyright © 1996, 2004, 2007 by Tyndale House Foundation. Used by permission of Tyndale House Publishers, Inc., Carol Stream, Illinois 60188. All rights reserved. Scripture quotations marked NIV are from THE HOLY BIBLE, NEW INTERNATIONAL VERSION®, NIV® Copyright © 1973, 1978, 1984, 2011 by Biblica, Inc.® Used by permission. All rights reserved worldwide. Scripture quotations marked ESV are from The ESV® Bible (The Holy Bible, English Standard Version®). ESV® Permanent Text Edition® (2016). Copyright © 2001 by Crossway, a publishing ministry of Good News Publishers. Scripture quotations marked KJV are from the the King James Bible, which is in the public domain. Scripture quotations marked MEV are from the Modern English Version. Copyright © 2014 by Military Bible Association. Used by permission. All rights reserved.

Cover and book design by Timothy J. Chambers, TimothyChambers.com
Compiled, illustrated, and edited by Timothy J. Chambers.

Discover inspiring *Seeing Beautiful* info, coloring pages, and more at
SeeingBeautiful.com

Printed in China
17 18 19 20 21 5 4 3 2 1

For Kim—
My best friend. Life with you is truly beautiful.
My words and brushstrokes would lose their
purpose without your smile.

Also to our mothers, who taught us to laugh,
Dad, my favorite artist and teacher,
and to Lindsie, Drew, and Chloe—you are indeed a joy!

Many thanks to the friends—from bankers to receptionists—who
provided candid feedback on the book during its creation. Picturing
you reading and coloring it guided me along the way. I hope you
find the book to be a source of relaxation, joy, and inspiration.

INDEX OF ART TIPS

Bookmarks and note cards	100
Circle shading	16, 80
Color over shaded illustrations	13, 22, 87
Color, achieving depth	76
Color, complements	38, 70
Color, dark scenes	84
Color, light to dark	78
Color, metallic	44
Color, monochromatic	17
Color, sunshine	72
Coloring page styles	22
Crosshatching	16, 63
Feathering	16, 80
Getting started	16
Pace, relaxed	14
Scrap paper, useful	18
Shading, circles	16, 80
Shading, crosshatching	16, 63
Shading, feathering	16, 80
Shading, shiny objects	98
Shading, styles	16, 48, 63, 80
Technique, pencil pressure	87
Texture	32
Tints, scales	28
Values, achieving depth	24
Values, scales	28

CONTENTS

A Very Unique Coloring Book 8
Meet the Artist 11
Introduction 12

   1. Beauty 14
   2. Change 26
   3. Perspective 36
   4. Imagination 46
   5. Vision 58
   6. Joy 68
   7. Perseverance 76
   8. Action 86
   9. Dessert 96
  10. 17°—Tim's Story 105

About Iguana Art Academy 112

A VERY UNIQUE COLORING BOOK

I am thrilled that you've joined me on the journey of seeing beautiful. I hope you find peace and encouragement as you color. I have chosen to take a slightly different path for this coloring book. I think you will appreciate the unique features, and find increased pleasure as your creativity capabilities grow.

Launch your creativity! My aerospace friends tell me that rockets and planes require a good portion of their fuel just to get off the ground. Art can be the same way—it takes some oomph to get going! This book provides plenty to get you into orbit.

Cherries, mandalas, Mars, vineyards, birds and bees. You'll find a variety of illustration opportunities to suit your mood and time—from graphic mandalas to memory-catching scenes to beautiful creatures of air and sea, not to mention a few desserts (all in good taste).

Fluffy Pancakes. Typical coloring pages are flatter than a flapjack! Flip through the pages and you will notice that some illustrations are done in ink, others in pencil. The pencils help you create colorings with a 3-D, breathable, organic feel. If you're in the mood for a more graphic feel, dive into the inks! To help give your work a sense of depth, I have added just enough shading to give you a head start to achieving beautiful, colorful, three-dimensional illustrations. Turn to page 22 to learn more.

You've got class! With this book you receive a free interactive **Seeing Beautiful Coloring Book Course** at IguanaAcademy.com. Learn new techniques as you color step-by-step the illustrations in this book. Iguana courses fit your schedule, available to you 24/7. Find details inside the back cover.

Inspiration! Be replenished with words of inspiration and encouragement about the journey of life as you color. Thought-provoking, heart-inspiring words to relax you while you enjoy the peace of creative flow.

Art Tip

Your Guide to the Universe. Okay, maybe that's overstating it. However, you do have in your hands a guide to great coloring. I've provided **Art Tips** throughout the book to help you express your creativity, including tips on shading techniques, monochromatic (one-color) shading, achieving vibrant and coordinated color, adding energy to your drawings, and more. Plenty of guidance to inspire your creativity and make coloring fun.

 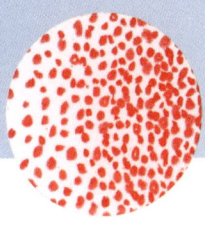   

 **The blank page monster...vanquished!** I have added shading to some illustrations to help you get going, to help cast a vision that you can run with! Go ahead and color right over the shading. The added shading helps you get your darks quicker, just like in the pancakes on page 22 (check out the Art Tip there to learn more about this helpful feature).

Inspiration from the stars. I have included art from the museums of some pretty good colorists! Soak up Van Gogh's *Starry Night* and you will never look at the night sky the same again. Join artists throughout the ages who copied the masters before them to expand their creative borders.

Starry Night by Vincent Van Gogh

 **Health and beauty.** Don't tell anyone, but sitting down and coloring are actually good for your health! Studies show that coloring can reduce anxiety, create focus, bring more mindfulness, develop hand-eye coordination, be a means of expression, and more. And no harmful side effects!

Share the joy. Create beautiful gifts to share when you color the bookmarks and note cards included. Nothing says "I care" like a beautiful, hand-drawn work of art. You'll find even more colorables at SeeingBeautiful.com.

 **Colorful friends.** Find kindred spirits who also enjoy coloring and growing. Discover encouragement, ideas, coloring tips, and talk shop with new friends at **SeeingBeautiful.com** and at **Facebook.com/seeingbeautiful**.

Shelly and Her Daughters, 42" x 44" Oil on Linen by Timothy J. Chambers
Enjoy more of Tim's paintings at TimothyChambers.com

MEET THE ARTIST

Tim Chambers is an international award-winning artist, having been a professional portrait and landscape artist for over twenty-five years. Tim grew up in a home where his father began his professional art career as an illustrator in Chicago for many years before adapting to a successful career in portrait painting. Tim enjoyed watching his dad work, and to this day practices the lessons he heard and saw in that wonderful place.

Since he was a little boy, Tim had his sights set on being an artist. It wasn't until his kindergarten teacher discovered that he had hearing loss that he began his journey of wearing hearing aids and being different from the rest of the kids. Doctors told his parents that his hearing loss was due to being prematurely born a month ahead of schedule in 1963, but the true puzzle piece to that mystery was finally discovered at the age of thirty when he was officially diagnosed with Usher Syndrome Type III, a genetic disease that steadily robs a person of their hearing and sight.

Imagine being at the pinnacle in your rapidly succeeding career, on the heels of winning top place at an international portrait competition, beating out fourteen hundred competitors from around the world, only to be told you're losing your hearing and sight, and with no known cure. Add to that a doctor with poor bedside manner who conveyed that Tim would soon lose all his vision and hearing, and thus better quickly find another career.

It was a devastating diagnosis that led Tim to a two-year fight against what he feared most—going completely deaf and blind, and never being able to create again.

Through a deepening of his faith and buoyed by the love of his family, Tim has walked the scary path of what-ifs and endured the changes brought on by the gradual loss of hearing and sight. He has continued to produce his finest work to date despite having only 17 degrees of vision remaining, and a 70 percent hearing loss. Those who know him agree that he lives a remarkable life of gratitude and humility, while being an encouragement to others, and having an authentic faith and a great sense of humor. Among his favorite quotes is one by Jonathan Swift: "May you live all the days of your life!"

Having been Tim's friend for almost forty years and his wife for almost thirty, I can confidently say that Tim truly lives life to the fullest, even on the hard days, always giving thanks for the gift of life.

Creating this coloring book has been a welcomed, fun adventure for Tim, and an excursion from an intense, fruitful career of portrait painting. Tim invites you to sit back with your favorite beverage, perhaps your favorite music of choice, and maybe joined by a friend or two, and enjoy the journey he's created for you to ponder as you consider what living a life of peace, joy, and encouragement looks like through creating beauty in your book. May you live all the days of your life,

Kimberly Chambers

INTRODUCTION

"Vision is the art of seeing things invisible." —Jonathan Swift

Did you know that a hawk's range of vision spans 290 degrees? That's a mere 60% more than our 180°! I'm an artist, so I've got terrific vision, right? Uh, no. My visual range comes in at 17°, less than 10% of what you probably can see, deeming me legally blind. If we were chatting over coffee, and I'm looking at your eyes, your chin disappears, along with everything else outside that little 17° circle. But I see enough to see beautiful.

And beauty is what I hope to help you create and see and experience. I've designed this book as if we were companions on a journey. Rather than give you blank pages with a few lines on them and say "Good luck!", I've provided practical art tips to guide you, and as no journey is taken without nourishment, I've brought along some encouraging thoughts to nibble and ponder upon along the way.

I have taught a lot of students, and I've found that they can fly once they catch a vision of where to go. It only takes me a minute or two of working on their drawing for them to say "Aha! I get it now! Okay, I can take it from here." That's the approach I offer in this book. I have added shading and color on some drawings, inviting you to jump in and take it from here. Yep, just lay your colors right on top. You'll be amazed at how good your drawings look! You will also find plenty of art tips along the way that will help you soar to new heights in your creativity.

I'm thankful for the gift of art. I can't imagine doing anything else. But I've discovered a greater gift: weakness. Instead of hardship destroying me, it has shown me beauty I never would have discovered in ease or strength. We can see beautiful not just in spite of life's challenges, but because of them. Consider this book a companion for this (sometimes perilous) journey called life. As a friend, I've also shared a few things I've learned (the hard way). I hope you find them helpful for your journey. Relax, reflect, color, enjoy, and smile as you discover peace and beauty along the way.

Soar with color

Throughout this book I have included illustrations in a variety of formats, including shaded pencil, like the hawk above, to add a fun twist to your coloring adventure. All this hawk needs to really soar is your color!

The coloring to the right was done by coloring with colored pencils right over the shaded drawing above. I've taken the guesswork out of what to shade light or dark; all you have to do is add your color to end up with a life-like drawing. Enjoy!

BEAUTY

"The best and most beautiful things in the world cannot be seen or even touched—they must be felt with the heart." —Helen Keller

What a gorgeous day for a wedding! Everything sparkles under the warm sun, a gentle breeze wisps the clouds across the pristine sky. The outdoor ceremony has everyone smiling at the beautiful bride and groom, as happy as the day is bright.

You smile as you take in the beauty. From the moment you arrived, you noticed how perfect everything is. The venue's beautiful entry, the gently curving drive under a cozy canopy of trees painting a kaleidoscope of colors—yellow sunlight deckled among purple, blue, and green shadows across the gravel driveway leading past magnificent green lawns, herbal gardens, and park benches nestled under towering oaks. There is a three-tiered fountain cascading water to the pond below. Beside it is a lovely French restaurant, its manicured grounds teeming with flowers in full bloom of soft pinks, pristine whites, and soft yellows, myrtles line the walkways. You close your eyes and breathe in the sweet fragrance in the air.

Stepping inside the restaurant, you enjoy another feast for the eyes: tables with beautiful centerpieces, glistening silver, sparkling glasses and china neatly set upon crisp starched linen. The tables are arranged perfectly throughout the large room, beautifully lit with large windows that overlook the gardens. Exquisite chandeliers cast a warm glow. What a lovely setting.

What is astounding is that all this beauty, organized so perfectly with not a flaw to be found, didn't happen by accident. The wonderful calm that you are enjoying was preceded by a torrent of energy. The beautiful reception hall was bare, workers scurrying every which way preparing, vacuums roaring, dishware rattling. Outside, workers were mowing, cultivating, clipping.

In other words, it wasn't always this way. Before tranquility and order was seeming chaos.

I think that life is often this way. Our eyes and hearts are drawn to the reward—the winning, the relaxing, the success. Yet we know that the things we admire come with perseverance. We till the soil, prepare the food, work out the design, plan for the trip. We anticipate and enjoy the fruits of the persevering through the waiting, the labor, the longing.

And oh, how worth it it is! Such a beautiful wedding feast awaits!

Enjoy a relaxing, slow-paced stroll

As you are coloring, breathe easy, take your time, let patience accompany your coloring. For this illustration, imagine the colors of a sunny day: greens, yellow-greens, warm yellows and oranges, and a delightful blue sky. You can look in the Art Tips Index at the back of the book for a list of topics to guide you as you go along your journey. Relax, and enjoy the view!

Getting started

Starting off with blank paper or canvas can be incredibly daunting, even if you're a professional! To keep things simple, let's start by shading a bunch of circles (aka grapes!).

- *How shall I begin?* I like to get warmed up by starting simple. That means I don't tackle anything difficult, but will sharpen pencils, lay out my paints, and start with something simple and safe that isn't the focal point, such as the background.

- *Any advice on color?* If color is new to you, check out the Art Tip on page 38 for a quick lesson on how colors work together. I recommend starting off by doing a monochromatic (one-color) drawing with black or your favorite color. This eliminates the complication of coordinating colors and allows you to focus instead on tone (values). See my example below of the grapes using one color (black) in various shades from light to dark.

- *How do I obtain the different value shades?* Although there are many shading techniques (which I will share throughout the book), let's start with three simple techniques—**feather**, **crosshatch**, and **circles**—demonstrated and explained below. Each row shows the process from start to finish, left to right.

Row 1: Feather Style. Hold your pencil at the opposite end from the tip for gentle control, easing the pressure to gradually get lighter. I start shading near the edge where I want darker value (tone) towards the lighter area.

Row 2: Crosshatch Style consists of multiple layers of straight lines, each layer drawn a different direction than the others. The more layers of lines, the darker the value (tone). As you proceed, draw lines where you need more color and tone.

Row 3: Circles. Lots of 'em. I start by holding my pencil opposite the point to achieve a delicate touch. As I add more circles where I want darker tones, I apply more pressure. For the lighter tones (highlight area), I apply less pressure.

You can watch and learn these techniques in more detail in your free Color Beautiful online course at Iguana Art Academy. See page 112 for details.

Color is beautiful... And so is black and white and gray. The drawing to the right was done with only a graphite pencil. You can create a simple single-color drawing with any of the illustrations in this book using a regular graphite pencil or a single color of choice. Artists throughout the ages created beautiful "value studies." The simplicity of thinking only of values (light/dark shading) can make for a relaxing experience.

Repeat after me... There may be a lot of grapes here, but if you repeat the shading tips on page 28 for each circle, *voila!* Suddenly you have a beautiful cluster of grapes!

If we are ever to enjoy life, now is the time, not tomorrow or next year… Today should always be our most wonderful day.

Thomas Dreier

Scrap paper happiness

Your scraps can save you heartache and bring happiness? Yes! You've worked hard at a drawing, only to put down the wrong, unerasable color. Bummer!
1. Test your color ideas before you apply to your finished work. I recommend sampling two or more colors side by side until you find what you have in mind.
2. A clean sheet of paper placed under your drawing hand will keep your hand and work clean and smudge-free.

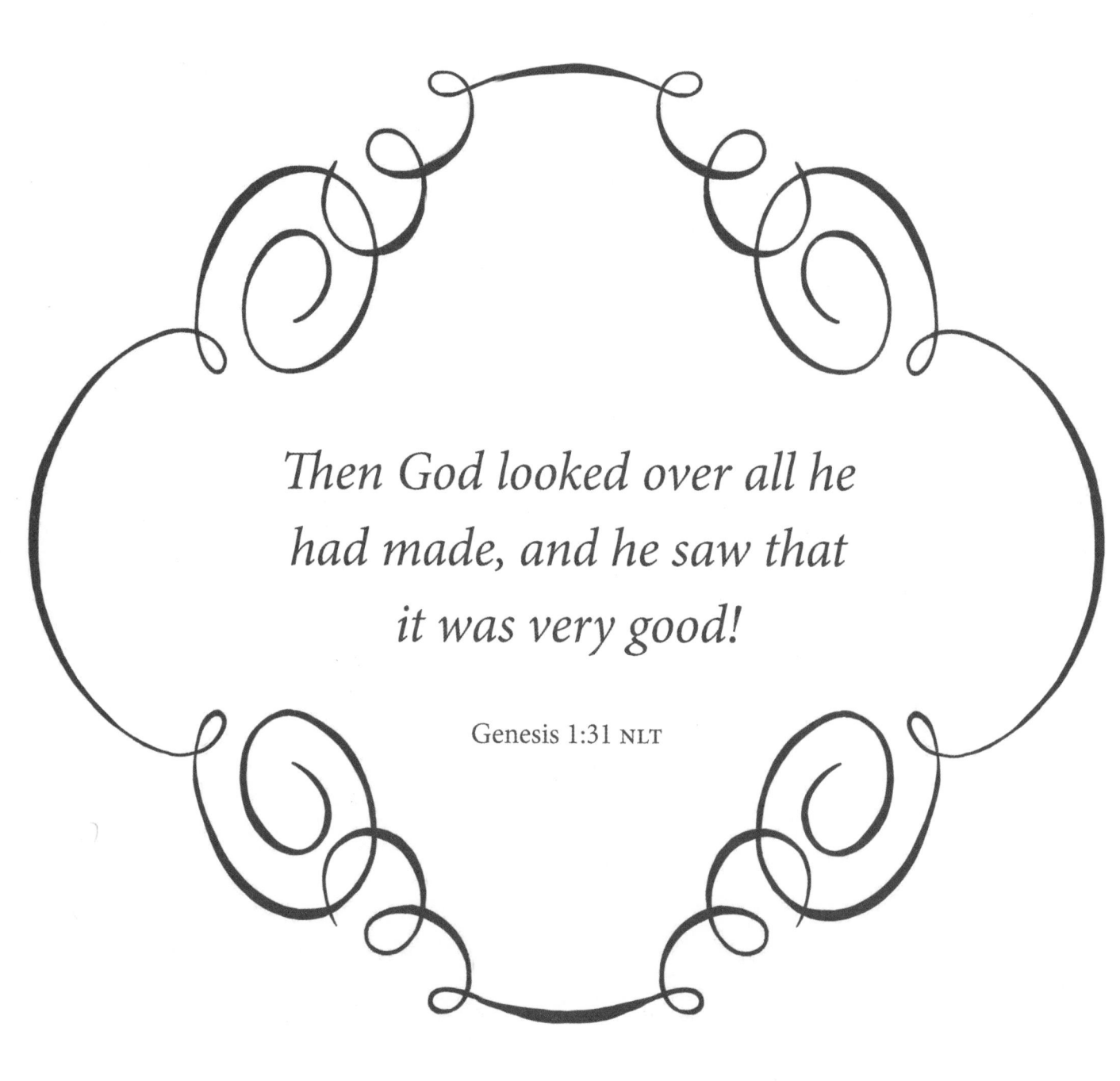

Then God looked over all he had made, and he saw that it was very good!

Genesis 1:31 NLT

 **Art Tip**

Sunflowers and pancakes in a variety of colorful flavors

You will find the coloring pages in this book come in a variety of styles to suit your mood. Some are drawn in ink outline, others in pencil, and still others are presented in a fun graphic format. I enjoy trying different approaches to my paintings, and no doubt you will enjoy trying something new as well.

If you're looking to keep things simple and mindless, then the inks and the graphics will suit you. If you're feeling a little bit more adventurous, then try the pencils; they invite a more intuitive approach with room to explore subtle shading and color interplay.

I have also chosen to provide shading to help you achieve depth and to assist in getting your motor running (a blank white page is intimidating even for the professional). The pancakes to the right illustrate how easy it is to build on the shading with your colors. It's almost like having a dancing partner to lead you along.

You will find art tips throughout the book, or use the handy index in the front of the book to help you find specific guidance for whatever you need help with at the moment.

Best of all, we've got a space reserved for you in the Color Beautiful course at Iguana Art Academy. Just navigate over to IguanaAcademy.com and enter coupon code *COLOR-BEAUTIFUL-FREE* at checkout to get the full course as a gift to readers of *Seeing Beautiful*. You will have a great time learning with other readers how to color beautiful!

You can color right on top of the shaded drawings! The shading gives you a head start and guides you where to shade.

The fountain of beauty is the heart.

Francis Quarles

Achieve depth and form with values

To give your colorings a real three-dimensional and natural feel, try implementing a variety of shading styles and stay mindful of value (tone) changes. A value scale is a great tool (learn more on page 28).

The best way to make water look like water is to think of it as a mirror, reflecting the sky above. That means that it will be a high value (#1–3) compared to the fountain and background. Only the sky will be as bright (unless, of course, you are doing a nocturnal scene). Make the fountain a few value steps darker (#4–6) so that it is a silhouette against the lively water. The fountain could be a warm gray compared to the cool white and light blue water. The trees could be a combination of dark greens, blues, and purples, on top of the gray.

For this illustration, I colored right over the black lines and gray background so that the static fountain and background would contrast with the bubbly, never-still water. It helps to ask *How is one thing different from another?* to help create separation and dimension. Try various shades of greens, blues, and browns together.

CHANGE

"Change is inevitable. Growth is optional." —John C. Maxwell

For almost every wonderful occasion such as the wedding we just enjoyed, there is usually a host of planning that preceded it. And with plans, there is usually a hiccup or two, or three… Have you ever had your plans interrupted? Your nest toppled? Of course you have. We all have. Whether it be your agenda toppled, financial hardship, expectations unmet, a relationship gone askew, illness, the loss of someone close, we've all experienced the letdown of plans gone astray. We affirm Robert Burns' verse from "To A Mouse": "the best-laid plans of mice and men go oft awry."

I had just won top place in an international portrait competition, featuring over 1,400 entries. I had known since a young age that I was going to be an artist when I grew up, and here I was living my dream. I figured it wasn't long before my paintings would grace the halls of Congress and the White House. I was only thirty years old.

About the same time, I went in for a routine eye exam, the kind I've had since I was eleven. This time, however, the physician's face showed concern. He said he noticed "irregularities" on my retina, and referred me to a retinal specialist. This was not what an artist wants to hear.

I went to the specialist, enduring a battery of tests. My wife and I awaited the results in a cold examination room. The doctor opened the door, glanced at me, and said, "You have Usher Syndrome, a combination of Retinitis Pigmentosa and hearing loss. It's degenerative, and you will lose your sight and your hearing." He saw the look of surprise and disappointment on my face and scoffed "Why are you surprised? You must have known." I said "No, I never knew. I figured I didn't see well in the dark, that's all, and had been told that my hearing loss was due to premature birth." "Well, you have RP." was his retort.

It was a gut punch that sucked the wind right out of me. This can't be happening. Not to me. My life is just getting started with great things ahead. Take my hearing; but my eyes? No. Please, no.

I had brought my portfolio displaying my award-winning paintings. Thinking the doctor would respond with encouragement and compassion once he saw my skill set, I said "Here's what I do. I paint portraits for a living," and handed him my portfolio. He flipped through a few pages, and with all the warmth of a surgeon's scalpel, said "Huh. Better find another profession," and walked out of the room.

Ugh. As blunt a blow as I've ever felt. Seeing my despair, his assistant turned to me and apologized for the terse prognosis, filling me in on other facts about my eyes. The wind had gone out of my sails. Quickly, my best laid plans went awry, poof, gone. My worst fears set in.

I didn't sleep well that night. Actually, I didn't sleep well for the next two years. I would wake up in a cold sweat, fearful that I was going to end up relegated to the corner of the house—forgotten, deaf, and blind. I would be nothing but a shell of the creative person I once was.

Was I to become useless? Will I ever be able to go after life, engage with people, explore new things. I see and think and live life creatively, visually, artistically. I live, I move. Was that going to be taken away from me?

See a shaded coloring page of Reed and Candle *on page 87.*

A bruised reed he will not break, and
a smoldering wick he will not snuff out.

Isaiah 42:3 NIV

Nine values and tints to bring life to your art

Here is a simple exercise that is a great way to get warmed up, build up shading skills, and discover the many values and tints in your pencils. Color each strip below matching the color guide at the bottom. Working with a gentle, not too heavy touch, start by filling in square #9 as dark as your color will allow. Then do square #2 slightly darker than white (#1 stays paper white). Then go back to the dark end and make #8 slightly lighter than #9. You know what's next—make #3 slightly darker than #2. Then make #7 slightly lighter than #8, #4 slightly darker than #3, #6 slightly lighter than #7. Finish up with #5, hopefully fitting nicely between numbers 4 and 6!

If there are any sudden "jumps" from one square to the next, adjust accordingly. Keep in mind it is better to start off a little too light and then go darker if needed than to try and go lighter with colored pencils, as they don't erase easily. You can repeat this exercise on scrap paper with any of your colors to discover the broad range of values and tints available to you.

Artists think about an object's values—its lightness and darkness—to create a sense of dimension. We use tints (color mixed with white) and shading (color mixed with black) to bring our drawing to life. With colored pencils, we "mix" in white by letting the paper show through, and darks with black or other dark colors. Sound like fun? It is!

Lightest (white) to darkest tone of your black or graphite pencil, starting with square #9 (darkest):

| 1 | 2 | 3 | 4 | 5 | 6 | 7 | 8 | 9 |

Lightest (white) to darkest tone of a blue:

| 1 | 2 | 3 | 4 | 5 | 6 | 7 | 8 | 9 |

Lightest (white) to darkest tone of a red:

| 1 | 2 | 3 | 4 | 5 | 6 | 7 | 8 | 9 |

Lightest (white) to darkest tone of a green:

| 1 | 2 | 3 | 4 | 5 | 6 | 7 | 8 | 9 |

The best-laid plans of mice and men go oft awry.

Robert Burns

Life can seem like a mess, but a little color can make it beautiful.

Art Tip

Express energy with texture

Students often ask me "How will I know when I am done with my painting?" I always answer with "When you have achieved your concept—what you set out to say." No use going on talking when you've made your point! When coloring, there are a variety of ways you can apply your colors to express what you want to say.

    I enjoy trying different methods and looks, from the usual smooth look to dashes to zig-zags. Consider what you aim to convey with your artwork. I believe good art has a purpose, much the same way writing has a purpose. When you write a sentence or paragraph, you have something in mind, right? Put the same principle into practice with your art. Look at the piece overall, or the section you're working on, and ascribe an adjective to it.

    In this illustration, I aimed to convey the feeling of a life weathered by the winds and trials of many seasons. I wanted to show the cause (the winds), the effect (the bent tree), and the result (bent, but not broken). Now it's up to you to decide what colors and texture will carry that even further. A hot wind (reds and yellows)? Or the cold blustery winds of winter (blues and violets)?

    Here are two ways that I experimented to capture the energy and movement of the wind in *Weathered Tree*. I followed the wind patterns, using the gray undertone. In the first one, I went with all dots and dashes, using two shades of blue. On the other, I created sweeping lines to complement the dots, using blue and violet.

    Try different textures and colors on a sheet of scrap paper to see what grabs you. I'd love to see what you come up with! Share your results with me and other readers on our Facebook page and at SeeingBeautiful.com.

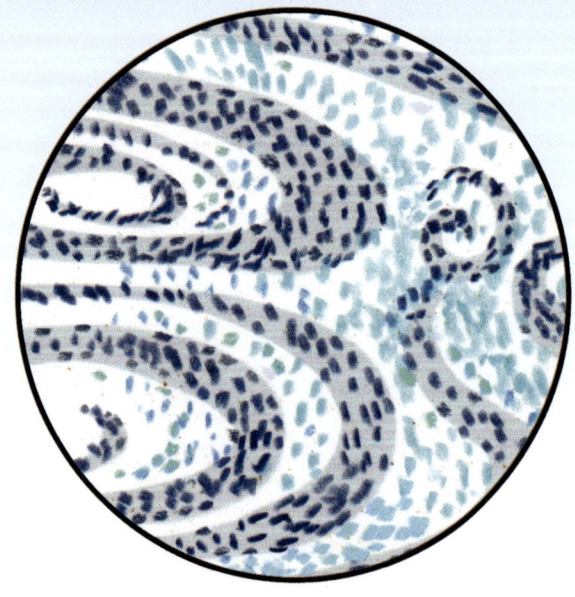
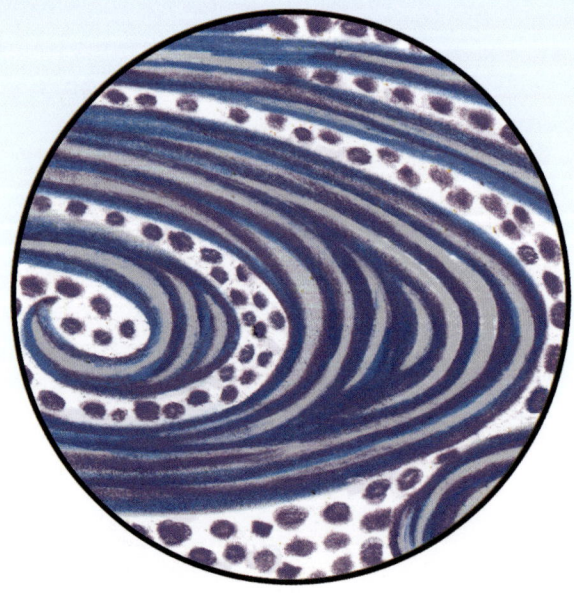

Through all the chaos and noise in the world, God can still hear the whispered prayer of his child.

Author unknown

PERSPECTIVE

*"A pessimist sees the difficulty in every opportunity;
an optimist sees the opportunity in every difficulty."* —Winston Churchill

"Window seat, please." I love flying. I still get tickles of excitement looking out the window at the land 30,000 feet below. Houses dot a patchwork quilt of farms with cotton balls floating within arm's reach. From my view I could see different forecasts—one home enjoys sunshine while another's forecast is overcast skies.

A pilot friend shared an experience about perspective. He told of flying a small plane, watching a car stuck behind a semi on a long stretch of two-lane highway. He watched as the driver inched to pass the truck, but never had a long enough view ahead to do so safely. Yet, from his view in the air, the pilot could see what lay ahead. "Go ahead and pass," he wanted to yell to the driver.

Have you ever prayed *Show me what lies ahead. I just need to know what to expect, what to prepare for*? It may not even be the difficulty that scares us as much as the not knowing.

After my diagnosis, I was scared. I was experienced with overcoming, having been "different" because of being almost deaf. I overcame that with humor, by excelling in art, and having supportive and loving parents. But this time, I felt as if I had nothing to stand on. If I didn't have my art, who was I? I thought I knew my future and who I was. Humor, compassion, or cliché provided solace. I was disoriented, like being buried by a massive ocean wave, not sure which direction to swim for air.

I'm not alone in the struggle. Recently I read a story of a family dealing with a dire prognosis for their child afflicted with a rare genetic disease that causes degenerative brain damage with no cure. I consider the parents, with dreams of the beautiful life ahead for their little girl, only to receive word from the doctors that she will soon need their care around the clock as she loses the ability to speak, eat, walk, becoming bedridden. Completely opposite of the life they envisioned.

Is there anything we can do to prepare for the thorns and clouds that come? I have learned that beyond keeping perspective, we cannot. We don't want to squander the beauty and good of the moment for the sake of preparing for potential hardship, but at the same time we don't want to live unaware of the fragile balance. Just as easily as a day can go from sunny to cloudy, it can return.

Is the glass half full, or is it half empty? Perhaps the glass is too big, because our expectations are unrealistic or presumptuous. I may be trying to fill a glass that's just not mine to live. Some of us are given pitcher-sized mugs, while for others a shot glass of strong challenges is more than enough to handle.

The flip side to having too-big expectations is missing out on the joy of a good thing. Have you ever had a wonderful gift, but instead of enjoying what it is, you focus on what it isn't? Or you worry about all the ifs that come with something, and instead of trusting that God will provide who and what is needed, you fret, usurping the joy of the moment from yourself and from others. Your glass is too big. Just enjoy the drink and be satisfied. And no worries—you get unlimited refills.

It certainly would be nice to know what lay ahead for us. Tomorrow is promised to no one, but you do have today. Let your perspective be to embrace what you do have, so that you truly may live all the days of your life. For me, I had

to stop living in fear of losing my sight and instead live in celebration of the sight I woke up with. My circumstances are what they are, but *my perspective determines my focus...and my happiness.*

Use color to add wow!

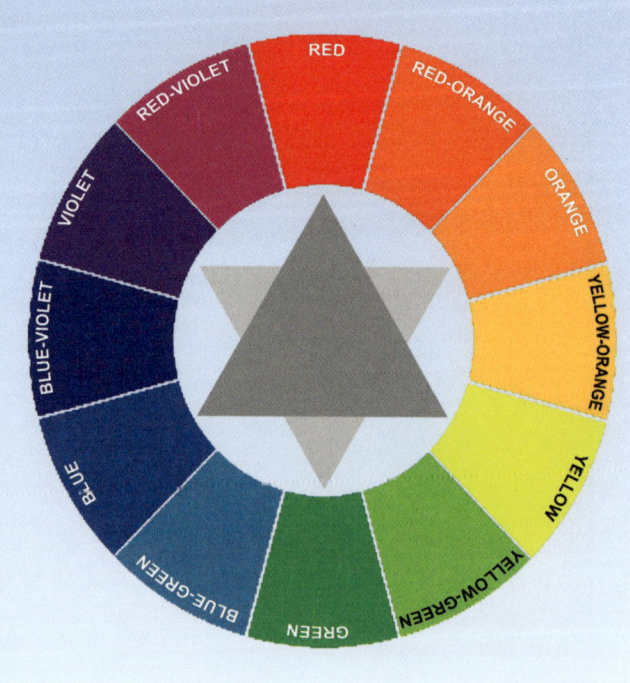

Learning a few basic principles about color can give you a powerful tool to create vibrancy and excitement in your art. The color wheel is a great tool to see what colors can do with each other. There are three primaries (colors that cannot be created with other colors: red, yellow, blue), three secondaries (colors created by mixing two primaries: orange, green, and violet), and six tertiaries (created by mixing a primary and secondary color).

Every color has a complementary color, which is its opposite on the color wheel. For example, red/green, blue/orange, yellow/violet. When placed next to each other, they are striking! Taken a step further, a color beside its grayed (muted) complement really stands out, as you can see in the combinations below. Notice how colors seem brighter, darker, bolder depending on what they're surrounded by. Keep this in mind when you start an illustration.

Experiment with your own combinations. We will talk about color in detail in your complimentary "Color Beautiful" course at IguanaAcademy.com.

Try your hand at combining a vibrant, pure color with a muted tone of its opposite (opposite across the color wheel).

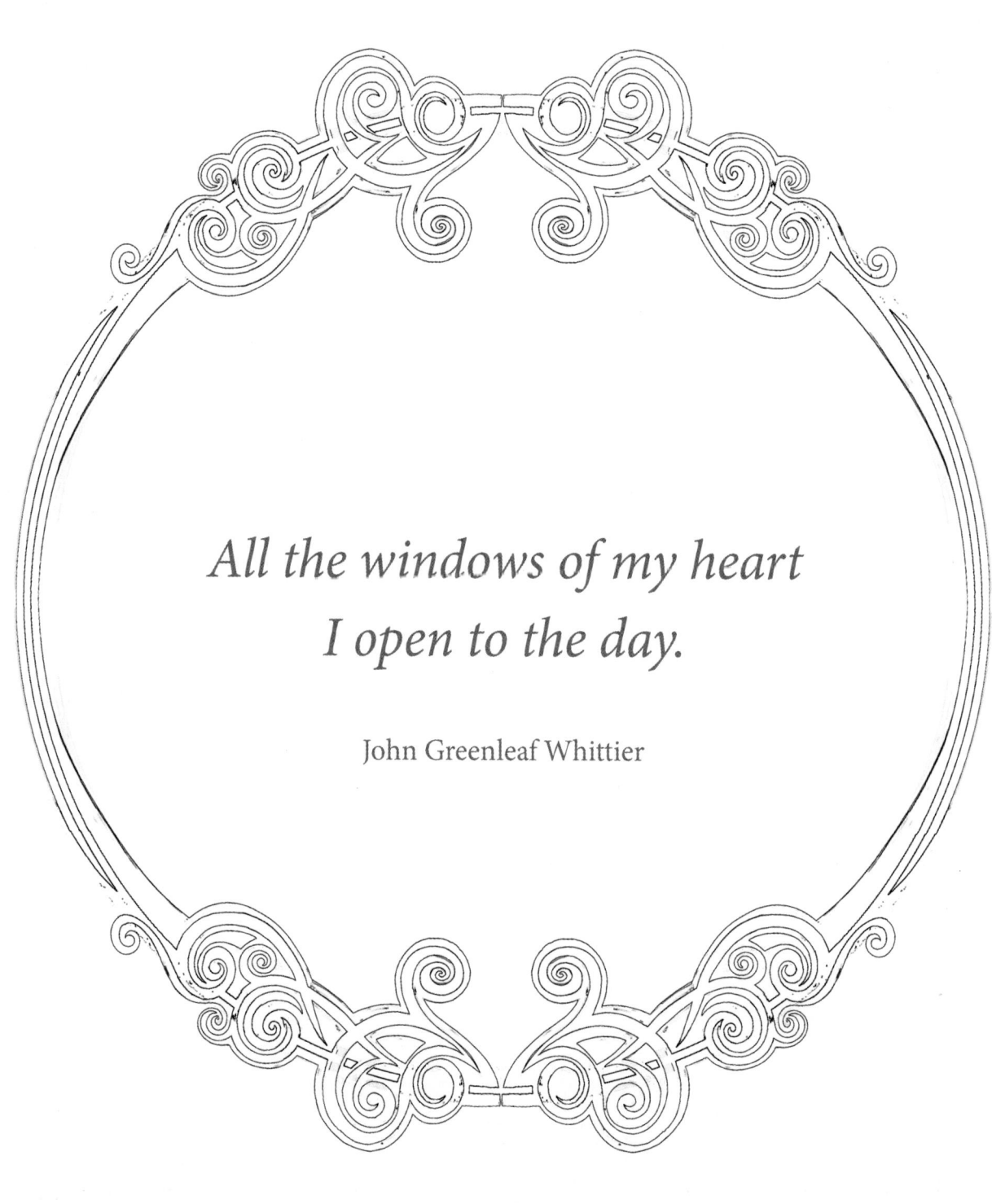

*All the windows of my heart
I open to the day.*

John Greenleaf Whittier

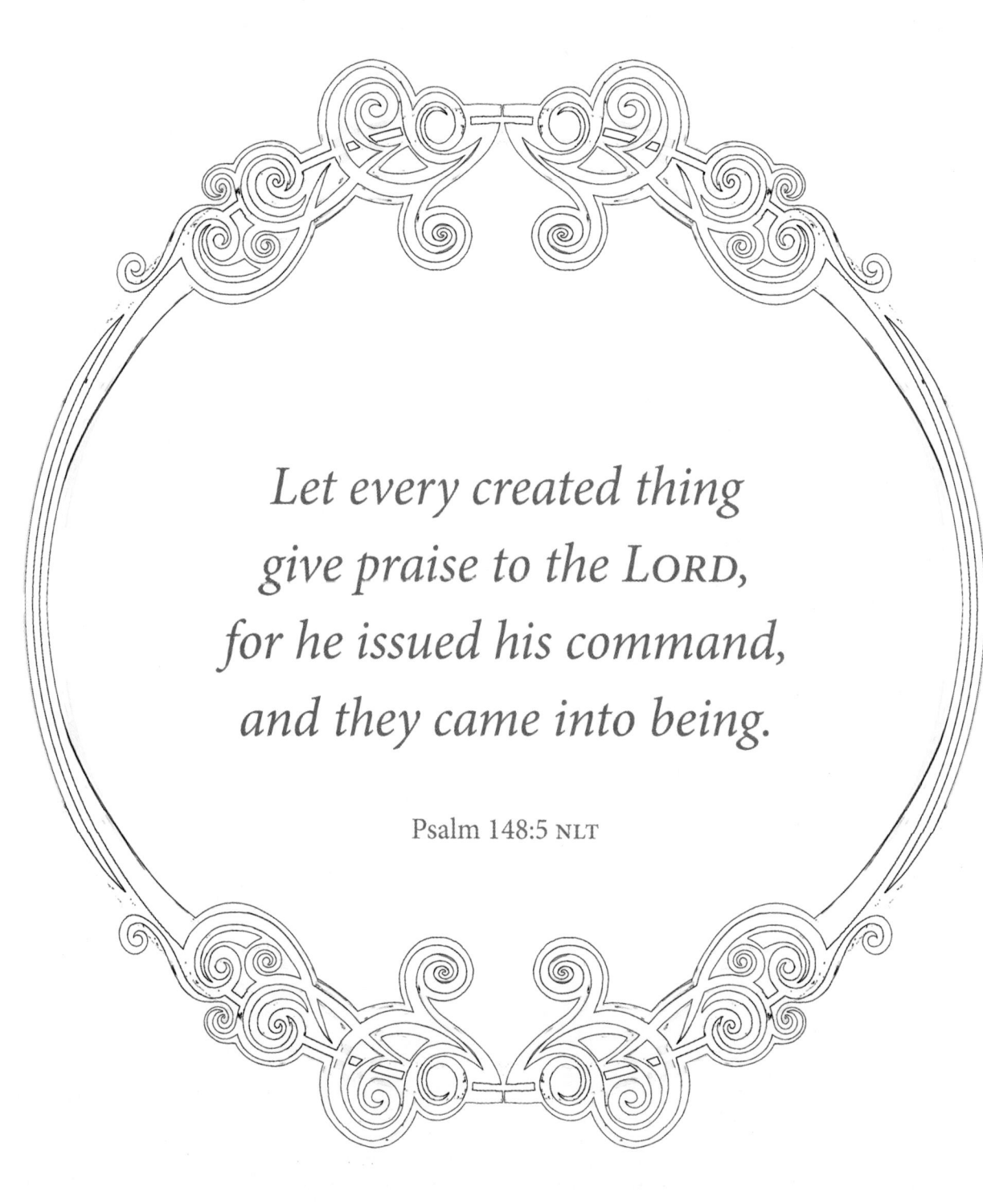

Let every created thing
give praise to the Lord,
for he issued his command,
and they came into being.

Psalm 148:5 NLT

Going for the gold

Austrian Gustav Klimt's famous painting *The Kiss* is unique in combining realism and abstract in one painting. If you are up for a challenge, I think you will enjoy the nuances of gold tones in this coloring. I have included the value shades in the illustration to help you capture the boldness of the shapes. Though the painting has many shapes and Art Nouveau designs, it is otherwise simple in composition and the number of colors and values used. How many different colors do you see in the detail below? If you have metallic gold and silver pencils, along with black, blue, red, yellow, and brown, you can obtain a fairly good result.

A few tips:
- Think layers. Metallic colors are influenced by the color immediately underneath. Notice that the golds on Klimt's robe vary. Some have a yellow tint, others more red, some warm (reds, oranges), some pale (light yellow or blue). Experiment on your scrap pad with different combinations.
- You can also make your blacks warm or cool by mixing (layering) black with dark maroons, blues, or purples.
- For the skin tones, I recommend a delicate approach to contrast with the fabric. Start lightly with yellow ochre, then add blush and pale colors.
- You can also make your blacks warm or cool by mixing (layering) with dark reds, blues, and purples.
- Keep your bright colors intense by keeping them pure and clean. Test on your scrap pad to find the perfect red, yellow, light blue or green.

The Kiss by Gustav Klimt, 1907

IMAGINATION

"A strong imagination begetteth opportunity." —Michel de Montaigne

Seventeen. That's my number. Yours is probably over two hundred, and that's a good thing. Mine is dangerously close to zero.

I am talking about vision, or more precisely, visual field—the span or range of vision from left to right, above you to below. If you were to spread your arms out wide with your hands slightly behind you, chances are you could see both hands while looking straight ahead, a spread of 180–200 degrees visual range. A hawk enjoys a sweet 240 degrees of peripheral vision.

Me? My peripheral vision has steadily decreased since I first found out I had Ushers. I have 17 degrees, about 10 percent of your vision. Two digits! If you and I were standing face to face enjoying a conversation, and I was looking you straight in the eye, I would not see your chin.

People ask me "Well, what is everything else, then? Black?" No, not black, not anything, only memory. What our eyes don't see, our magnificent brains fill in the gaps. We take quick mental notes to complete our 360 degree awareness. I just have to work a bit more to complete the picture. I guess you could say it's my imagination at work.

One of the most daunting things for an artist is a blank canvas. It is at once both an invitation to create anew, as well as a wall that towers over you, intimidating, almost taunting you to sum up the courage to dare ruin its simplicity. How often have people been paralyzed in the face of opportunity?

I see this played out at every art workshop. Students young and old stare at their blank canvas, afraid or unsure to "mess up" the pristine canvas with their strokes. Instead of thinking they will improve it with their handiwork, they fear they will move it to ruin.

Isn't that what Jesus' parable of the talents could be about? Three people were given skills. Two went out on a limb and made a difference. The other buried his opportunity for fear of failure. He was scolded while the other two were praised, not for success, I believe, but for action.

What do you do with the unknown? I believe that without imagination, we lose the excitement and potential of possibilities. Albert Einstein, a very smart fellow, concluded "Imagination is more important than knowledge." What wonderful things would happen in our lives if we let imagination reign over fear!

Windows are a wonderful opportunity for imagination. Two people can look out the same window and respond in completely different ways. I wonder who first thought of the idea of transforming a plain window into a work of art? The beauty of stained glass windows mesmerized me when I was a child; the colors, shifting in sunlight, kept me awake!

So, if you're seeing black or drawing a blank beyond what you can see, perhaps your imagination would benefit from exercise. Then again, you may be using your imagination more than you realize. You may be using it to draw up images using colors of fear, rather than colors of living. If someone asked you the question often asked of me: "What can you see?" … what do you answer?

Starry Night by Vincent Van Gogh, 1889

The heart set free with imagination!

Vincent van Gogh's *Starry Night* is an amazing example of letting your imagination express not only the yearning of your heart, but also the expression and energy of the creative universe. My goodness! Can you not just feel the splendor of that night? Bring your drawings to life with a variety of color and texture (see page 32). Experiment with creative ways to lay your color on your drawings, such as these examples below.

The heavens proclaim the glory of God.
The skies display his craftsmanship.

Psalm 19:1 NLT

IMAGINATION: Starry Night Thinking

Certainly, you are familiar with *Starry Night* painted by Vincent van Gogh in 1889. But there is more to this masterpiece than meets the eye. Artist Makoto Fujimura revealed Vincent's beautiful story in a commencement address at Biola University a few years ago.

I was surprised to discover that Vincent had desired to become a pastor, but the church rejected his plea. He then worked as an evangelist to the poor in the coal mines of Belgium, living among them in their squalor. Vincent was an intelligent man, a thinker; he spoke five languages and wrote fluently in three. Yet he was plagued with mental illness.

While he worked with the coal miners, he began to draw them. Though not formally trained in painting and drawing, yet he discovered that he could communicate visually more deeply his compassion for humanity and of God's presence than when from the pulpit. Art gave to Vincent a way to express his heart and mind, and to Vincent, Christ was the ultimate artist, writing that Christ "lived as serenely as an artist greater than all artists."

Van Gogh painted "Starry Night" in Arles, France. Yet the focal point of the painting, is a white Dutch Reformed church, which did not exist in Arles. Vincent painted his childhood church from memory. This painting, like much art, is as much about the artist as it is the subject depicted.

Makoto pointed out that "if you are to take out the church (place a pinky over the church) from the painting, the whole painting falls apart visually. It is the only vertical form, aside from the dominant cypress tree on the left, which juts out to break the horizontal planes. The cypress tree and the church are two forms that connect heaven and earth. Without the church, the cypress tree takes over the swirl of movement, and there's no visual center to hold the painting in tension between heaven and earth.

"Notice, too, that homes surrounding the church are lit with warm light, but the church is the only building in the painting that is completely dark. Herein lies Vincent's message: the Spirit has left the church (at least the building), but is alive in Nature. If you follow the visual flow of the painting, your eye will cycle upward, but still anchored by the church building. Our gaze will end up on the right upper hand corner, at the Sun/Moon. Notice it is not just a moon, or a sun, but a combination. Vincent wanted to show that the Spirit of God transcends even Nature herself, that in resurrection, in the New Earth and the new Heaven, a complete new order will shape things to come."

Don't you just love how imagination and creativity can express the heart and mind so beautifully? I encourage you to give flight to the inner groanings of your heart via creativity. As Vincent showed us here, there is something wonderful to be said beyond the obvious, and you just may find your heart's desire.

All things bright and beautiful,
All creatures great and small,
All things wise and wonderful,
The Lord God made them all.

Cecil Frances Alexander

There are no seven wonders of the world in the eyes of a child. There are seven million.

Walt Streightiff

I have the world's largest collection of seashells. I keep it on all the beaches of the world... perhaps you've seen it.

Steven Wright

VISION

"Vision without action is a daydream. Action with without vision is a nightmare." —Japanese Proverb

My wife and I noticed a pattern in our children when we began planning our next summer vacation. Their countenance brightened, their chatter increased, their steps lightened. Suddenly the glass was half full rather than half empty. Enthusiasm and motivation were up, and our home was full of good cheer.

They had a vision. They had something to be excited about long before they had anything in hand, before hope was realized. Vision reaches for something greater, beyond your reach.

There is a familiar adage "Where there is no vision, the people perish." (Proverbs 29:18 KJV). We are a race, unlike any other, that absolutely thrives on vision. We need it to rise in the morning, and we need it for a sweet rest at night. We raise children with a vision in mind, marriages begin and prosper with it. Vision drives us, and sometimes vision survives us when we are at our weary end. Even commerce and livelihood depend on it. Every sales pitch, every marketing plan, is predicated on casting a vision of what could be: "If you buy this thingamajig, you will be happier!" with the tiny disclaimer that says "This most likely will probably not be true for you. The people in this ad are paid actors."

Blind musician Stevie Wonder said "Just because a man lacks the use of his eyes doesn't mean he lacks vision." Though I often have chance meetings with furniture, lamp poles, and strangers that often leave bruises on my body or ego, I can still have great vision on a far more important level.

In the previous chapter, I talked about imagination. I can't imagine vision or hope without it! A great quote that gives teeth to imagination is "faith is confidence in what we hope for and assurance about what we do not see." (Hebrews 11:1 NIV). Faith gives wings for imagination and vision to take off and fly. You can sit in your chair and imagine, but faith turbocharges your imagination and gives you reason to move your feet towards the vision.

Faith creates action. Vision gives your faith something to grab ahold of. I know this for certain: I could not have moved past the despair I have felt without a combination of imagination, vision, and faith. Imagination spurs vision, but without the action based on the faith that I will see the imagination and vision realized, the two would fizzle as quickly as dew on a summer's day, and with that comes the discouragement of unrealized dreams.

As an artist, my life is all about vision. Before I even have laid brush to the canvas, I can envision the completed painting. A blank canvas is an invitation to explore, to take the mundane and make it beautiful.

It doesn't stop there, however. Ask my wife and she will tell you I am a man of ideas. I look around and see ideas of what could be. A dilapidated house, a barren field, the lack of ambiance at a restaurant—I can visualize what they could be.

I also know the power of visualizing upon my countenance, my outlook. Much as I don't set out to create a painting of disharmony and discord, I try not to think the worse of my circumstances. "Every year of my life I grow more convinced that it is wisest and best to fix our attention on the beautiful and the good, and dwell as little as possible on the evil and the false," said Richard Cecil.

I have seen the powerful effect vision can have on relationships. From strangers to spouses, what you see determines what you think and do. Do I see a stranger's glass half empty? Or do I presume to find the good and leave

the rest to the One who knows the heart and circumstances? It's amazing how people respond—in a good way—when you treat them like you're thankful for them. One of my favorite verses is an oft-overlooked one: "some have entertained angels unknowingly" (Hebrews 13:2 MEV). I am sure we've encountered angels looking a lot more like those forgotten and despised.

Marriage craves vision like a fish needs water. Are not wedding vows a commitment to a vision? I believe a promise is indeed a vision, and no vision is attained by signature or decree, but by journey. My own marriage is a recipe for fireworks: two strong-willed, passionate individuals who don't much like mediocrity, falsehood, pseudo peace. Exciting...and dangerous. However, a common vision and faith has saved us many times from ourselves. Believing in what can be rather than focusing on the current lack is the only way. Belief in the vision and the keeper of the promise.

Having a clear vision makes life more beautiful for yourself, your spouse, children, friends, neighbors, even strangers. Vision is never bland. When cast selflessly, it has a sweetness. When cast wisely and with the fires of hope, it can do amazing things. The history books are evidence of that.

What is your vision today? If you don't have one or two, strike a conversation with a young child and ask them the question. You just may awaken dormant vision-making skills.

Building on a foundation

Sometimes I find it easier to obtain richer colors and contrast by starting with shading before I lay down color. Get a head start to achieving the rich darks and three-dimensional look by using the shading provided for you in the illustration. I recommend building up the value (darkness) and intensity of your colors by starting out with light pressure then gradually building up to a heavier stroke for intense notes, such as on the radish shown here. Mix yellows into your reds to achieve bright reds, oranges, and greens to give your colorings a wonderful life-like vibrancy!

Stop to smell the flowers ... and the earth.
Taste and see its goodness.

Vision is the art of seeing what is invisible to others.

Jonathan Swift

Try your hand at creating a value scale using the crosshatching method. See pages 28 and 63 for helpful art tips.

1	2	3	4	5	6	7	8	9

Be a crosshatch master

The crosshatch shading technique is one of the oldest methods of shading. Since the early 15th century, artists used hatching (parallel lines of varying thickness) and crosshatching (parallel lines that cross each other) in drawings, etchings and engravings, including paper currency. Take a close look at your paper money and you'll see wonderful crosshatch engravings.

Crosshatch is one of the easiest forms of shading. Because it is a layering method of shading, one of the best things about it is that it doesn't require a lot of planning, which is great for the casual artist. You build up the shading gradually and stop when you like what you see.

The drawing at right is by Rembrandt van Rijn, created almost 400 years ago. If you look closely, you will see that it is made up entirely of lines! And you don't even need to know how to draw a straight line (not that that ever stopped any great artist).

Crosshatching is very straightforward, as you can see below. You start with a series of parallel lines in one direction, then add your next layer of parallel lines on top of the previous. You simply add additional layers wherever you want a darker value (see page 28 for more about values).

Try your hand at crosshatching with the value scale on the facing page. Start with a single layer on square #9, then add a layer over #9 and #8, then a third layer over squares 7, 8, and 9, and so on. We will cover this in your Color Beautiful course at Iguana Art Academy.

Man in Oriental Costume (detail) by Rembrandt, 1635

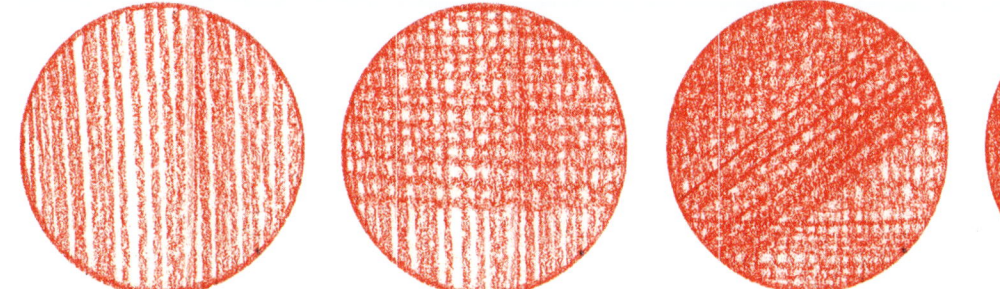

Start with one layer of parallel lines, then add additional layers of crossing lines to obtain darker shades.

63

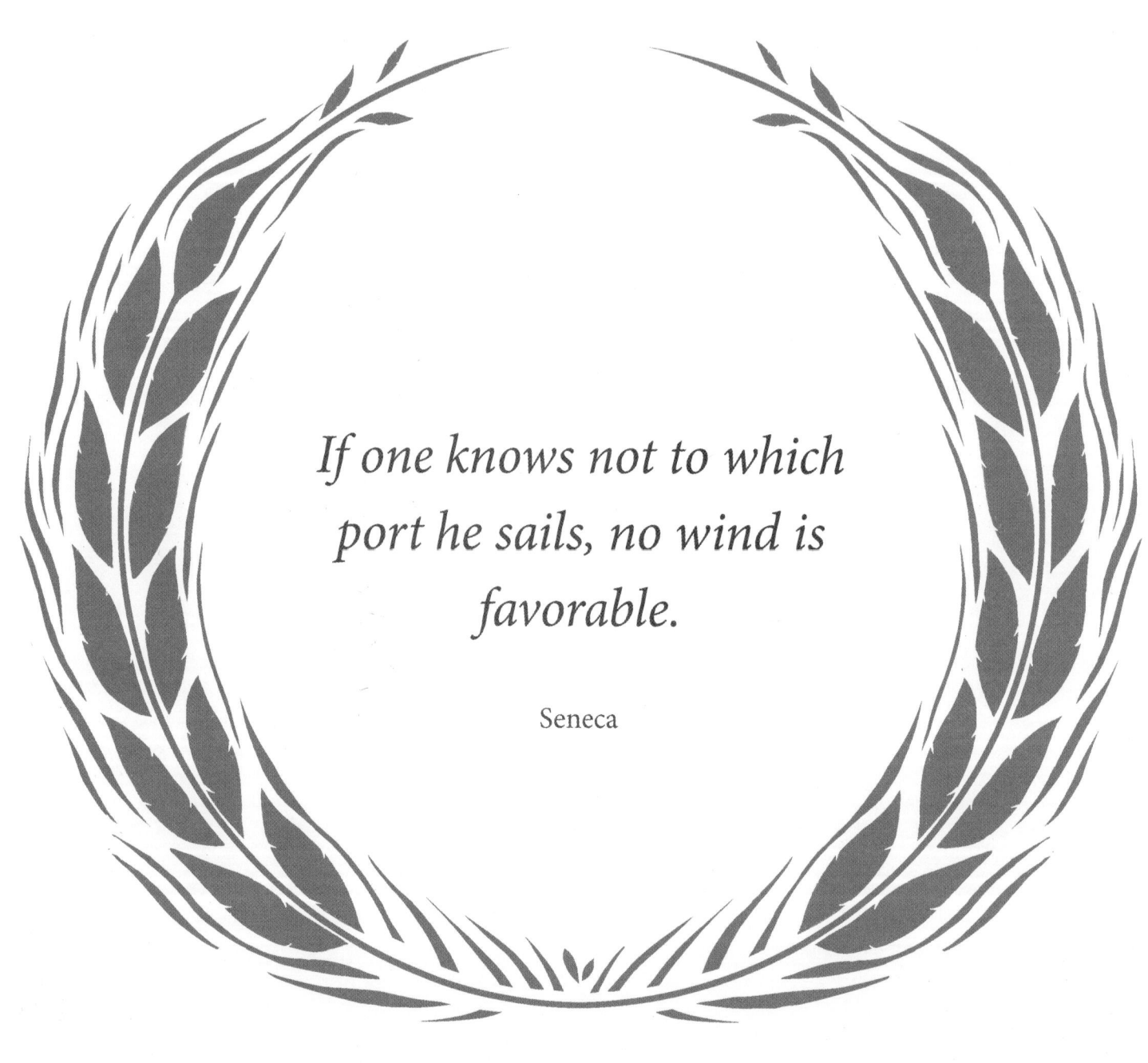

If one knows not to which port he sails, no wind is favorable.

Seneca

JOY

"Weeping may tarry through the night, but joy comes in the morning." —Psalm 30:5

Sunny mornings top my list of favorite moments. Everything is new. The night is gone, chased away by the warm yellow rays of sunshine. I wonder how many long nights have been endured solely on the hope of the coming dawn.

Just this morning as we pulled out of our driveway, I was given a gift—one I have received just about wherever I've been: sunshine.

To me, the morning sun's rays are happiness. Happiness painted across the streets, the lawns, the houses, like swaths of the most exquisite fabric in a queen's wardrobe. Glistening yellow splashed across the world. The pleasure splayed before me wasn't merely pretty houses or flower beds. It was simply the color of a new day spilled across the gray shadows of night. Weeping may stay the night, but joy comes in the morning.

What is joy? Have you thought about that? Is it the same as happiness? Webster defines joy as "the emotion evoked by well-being, success, or good fortune or by the prospect of possessing what one desires, a state of happiness or felicity, bliss, or a source or cause of delight." Essentially, the dictionary states that joy is an emotion, a feeling. But I think that's just a part of what joy is.

Emotions are fleeting. They can change in a blink, a shift of circumstances. I have found joy to be something deeper. I would even venture to say it is the opposite of depression, for both are more than mere emotions, and send their roots deep into our hearts. Maybe you have seen depression take hold of someone or yourself, like the flu takes hold of your physical body. You can feign happiness in either, but you cannot quench either with a mere change of circumstances. A dear friend who knows well the despondency of depression, remarked, "Joy is the abundance of the soul and depression is the depletion of the soul."

Pastor and author John Piper defines joy as "a good feeling in the soul, produced by the Holy Spirit." I find this interesting because it elevates joy beyond the physical and the mental. He says its source is not manufactured or contrived by us, but by someone beyond us—the Spirit of God. This helps me explain the staying power of joy—that it prevails through thick and thin, sun or rain, high and low. It also reminds me fruit starts with a seed. The Gardener prepares, plants, sends the rain and the sun.

There is a distinction, though, between the feelings of the emotions compared to the feelings of the soul. Even when you're weary from loss, pain, illness, or disappointment, joy can remain. This is because the source of joy is not you or circumstances, but the eternal God, who is steadily joyful. No matter your circumstances or emotions, you can still experience the faithful, peaceful presence of joy within.

Piper also states that joy finds its fullness when we delight in our Maker. Kind of cyclical, I know, but that too makes sense, doesn't it? That something good is more good when it delights in something good? Seems so obvious it makes me smile.

Joy trumps happiness. I discover this principle daily. The state of my eyesight is a little worse each day. Yet I am happier today than ever as I put more and more stock in the invisible treasures rather than what I can see, hear, taste, touch, smell, and buy. Joy gently but firmly pushes back the gray shadows of the night.

Find a photograph of a classic car to see how chrome has crisp color edges compared to the gradated shades of metal.

Joy is intrinsic, a wellspring from the deep that evokes happiness and delight. We can't manufacture it. Like geysers and hot springs, its source is not itself. For me, that source is resting in that Someone greater than all my circumstances. For me, that is Christ, and even then it is a gift, not something gotten by wisdom, smarts, study, or hard work. Kind of like the true love of a parent—it's there for the taking, and blooms when returned.

With what little I see, I am glad that I can put aside the regrets of the past and the unknowns of the future and enjoy the beauty of a moment, a place, or a person. I can be too busy, but when I step off the whirlwind for a moment, catch my breath, I can breathe in the still, quiet peace that is joy. Sometimes I let fears or circumstances cloud my vision. But it only takes a moment to quiet the distraction and let joy spring forth. Though life may get harder, the joy can get sweeter.

How about you? Would you say you know joy as described here? When you slow down your thoughts, step away from your schedule, and turn off your phone, can you enjoy the tranquil peacefulness of joy? Can you taste and feel it in life's special moments, such as when you're loving someone or being loved or doing something that you love to do, when you know it's not the thing or the person that is giving you joy, but it's your soul striking a perfect chord with the God who loves and delights in you? I hope you know this joy. And if you don't, I know without a doubt that your Creator would find great pleasure in bearing this fruit in you. Ask what you seek, and let the master Gardener do his thing in and through you.

We've covered some great topics, but without the fruit of joy, is anything worth its price? "A joyful heart is good medicine, but a crushed spirit dries up the bones" (Proverbs 17:22 ESV). This is my wish for you—that joy would spring forth from your innermost being. Then, no matter what, you will see beauty wherever you may be.

More Complements!

Complementary colors are actually opposites (ironic, I know). When side by side, they play off each other and may feel like they vibrate with energy. Think orange/blue, purple/yellow, red/green, yellow-green/red-violet...exciting combinations!

To emphasize one color (and not its complement), have one be bold (full strength) and its complement a grayed, more neutral hue. For example, a strong orange next to a dull blue, or a strong red beside a pale green, as in the combinations at right.

Practice on scrap paper and then create an exciting design with this sphere using polite, I mean complementary, colors.

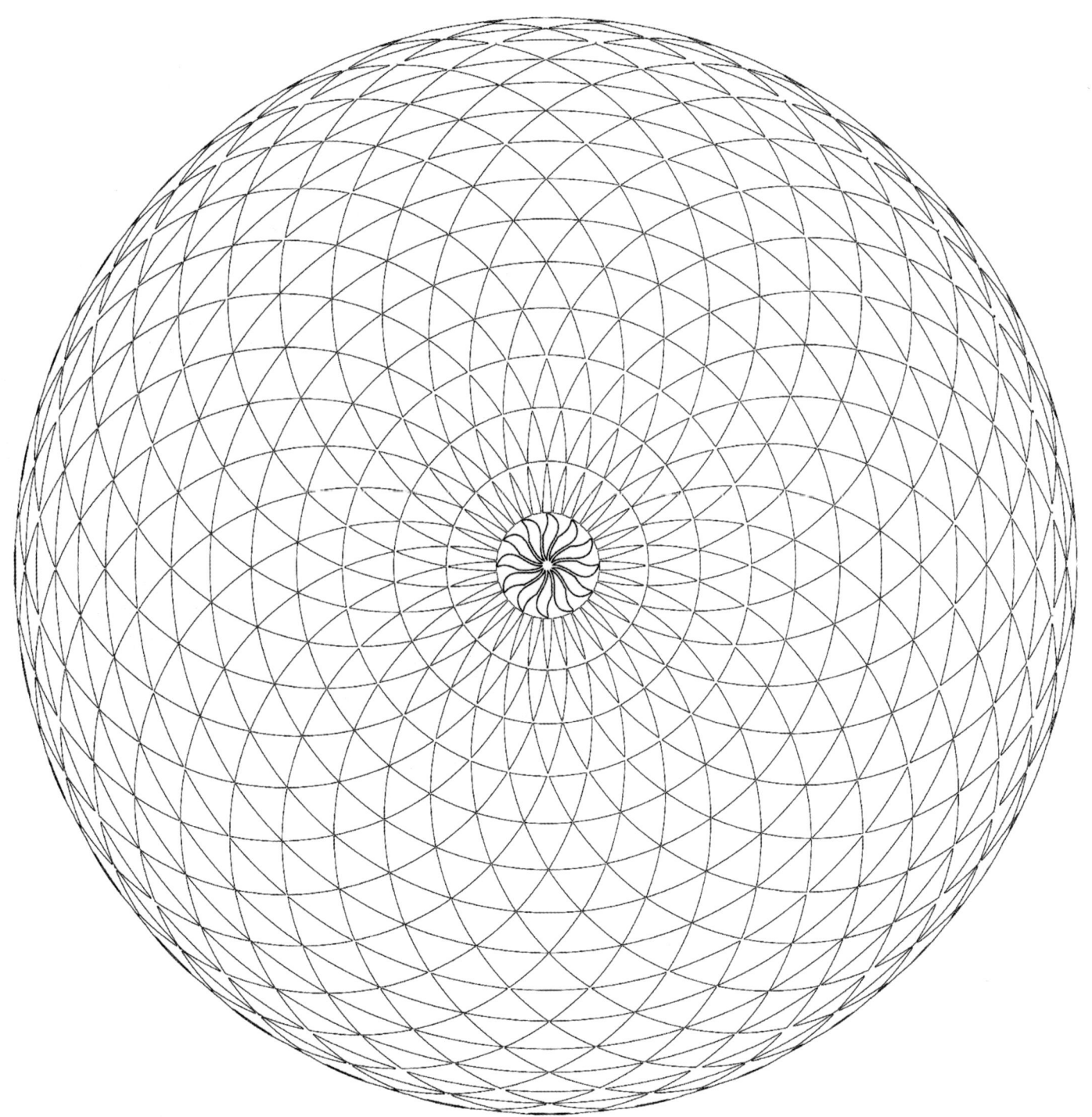

Coloring sunshine

If you have been doing any reading, you know how I feel about sunshine. I can't get enough of it. One of my favorite things to do is to paint landscapes in full sun. You don't need stunning vistas to find inspiration. This painting is just around the corner from our home, and I found delight in the play of colored roofs and greenery ablaze with the sun's bright warmth. See if you can capture the variety of colors that I see. You will make good use of your full color pencil palette, no doubt!

One way to get the variated colors is to shade with strokes, short marks, or dots that we learned in earlier Art Tips. This will enable the different, even opposite, colors to kind of vibrate next to each other yet work together to create the energy that we see in nature.

When coloring sunlit scenes, keep the sunny notes distinct from the shady notes both in value and in color tone. This will help you capture the warmth and bold presence of the sun.

Academy St. Roofs in Morning Sun by Timothy J. Chambers

My cup runneth over.

Psalm 23:5 KJV

PERSEVERANCE

"Determine that the thing can and shall be done and then we shall find the way." —Abraham Lincoln

I am not a chef or a baker, but I'm married to an excellent cook. The kitchen is my wife's canvas. She does with edible things what I do with poisonous concoctions of colorful paint. The funny thing is that we both know when an ingredient is missing or misused. In a blink Kim can spot a color on my canvas that just doesn't fit. I can do the same with one of her meals as well (though I have learned to be careful, as I really, really enjoy good home cookin').

I have learned that life has its own list of ingredients essential to both success and survival. There are a few: love, forgiveness, and perseverance. Strange combination, isn't it? We can get by without many things, but without those three, I don't think anyone survives for long. If we're interested in doing more than surviving, then add imagination and vision. Perseverance is to life what sugar is to a baker.

Dictionaries define perseverance as "the continued effort to do or achieve something despite difficulties, failure, or opposition: the action or condition or an instance of persevering: STEADFASTNESS." Synonyms include tenacity, determination, staying power.

Perseverance is vital to both surviving and succeeding. Sometimes it takes all we have just to stand, or to stay in place. Other times we are actively pursuing. Perseverance is what we do to fulfill Newton's First and Third Laws: we need it to keep going when forces try and knock us off our path. (I'd have paid attention in school if I knew how practical physics was!). When Newton's Third Law says stop, perseverance says "Not today!"

Perseverance has thus become one of my favorite and practical words. I have found it integral to things and achievements that I esteem. Liberty, freedom, independence. Perseverance plays a key role. Inventors, Olympians, parents,

Sierra Nevada by Edgar Payne

Going the distance

In the first half of the twentieth century, California painter Edgar Payne hiked throughout the Sierra Mountains capturing the dramatic beauty. No shortage of inspiration! And good exercise! As you color this illustration, note the subtle tones in Payne's painting. To get the feeling of distance, the darkest notes are reserved for the trees in the foreground.

climbers, researchers…they all persevere. We treasure things that are hardest gotten. It's easier for me to give up than to stay the course.

And when we give up, we don't stay where we are; we regress. It's just how things work. You need perseverance just to stay in place! I figure if I am going to work hard, why not work hard to get somewhere? Like forward, ahead. Imagination and vision come into play, like playmates to perseverance.

A worthy pursuit requires perseverance. First, we must start. Then we must continue. There are only two mistakes we can make: not starting and not continuing. Get those two right, and we'll get somewhere. It's a matter of making sure you're heading the right direction. Inspiration can get us started. Vision can point the way. Perseverance gets you across the finish line.

When our world is jarred, flipped upside down, our bearings are topsy-turvy, the wind is sucked from us, as I felt when told that I will lose my sight and hearing, or when there is no wind at all, we have a choice. We can wither and crawl into a hiding place, we can do nothing as if numb or paralyzed, or we can do something. Unless we resist, press on, fight, we regress. Taking the first step, establishing momentum, is hard, yet made easier if you have a vision in mind.

A clear vision helps perseverance, too. For when you are weary, and ready to give up rather than press on when things seem hopeless, having a clear vision will help you discern the voices that whisper for you to give up the fight. You will recognize truth from falsehood, hope from faithlessness, friend from deceiver, tough love versus self love. Perseverance recognizes the faithful friend that will walk with you through both the crisis moment or the long, fierce night, and sometimes carry you when you're on fumes. Perseverance is your mate on a tandem bicycle—moving to keep you balanced.

When I was diagnosed almost twenty-five years ago with losing my vision, the doctor told me to give up painting. A better and wiser doctor, when asked her opinion, said "Stop painting? Why would you do that? No, you paint until you cannot. Then you'll know what to do next." Two opinions, two opposite directions for my life. It was a choice between fear and vision. Which one do you think I chose? Hint: I see worse than ever, but am painting better than ever.

A faithful friend, who can find? Perseverance is an essential companion to living here and eternally.

Our colorful cosmos

For this illustration, consider how you might capture the drama of the celestial with rich darks and subtle color accents in the stardust. This view from the Hubble telescope gives a hint of creation's endless beauty.

Proceed from your lights to your darks. You can always go darker, but you cannot get the white of the paper or a light color once you have put down a dark color or tone.

A soft, light glow around stars will make them seem bright.

> *Look at the birds. They don't plant or harvest or store food in barns, for your heavenly Father feeds them. And aren't you far more valuable to him than they are?*
>
> Mathew 6:26 NLT

Circles and feathers

Here are two more methods of shading: feather and circles. By patiently building up layers, you can achieve beautiful, even tone and shading.

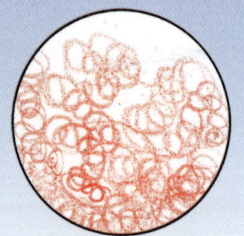 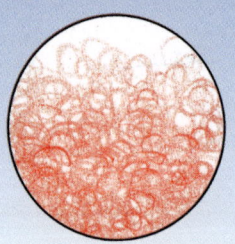 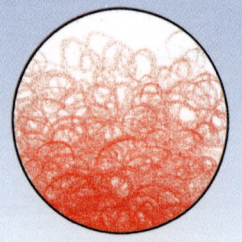  

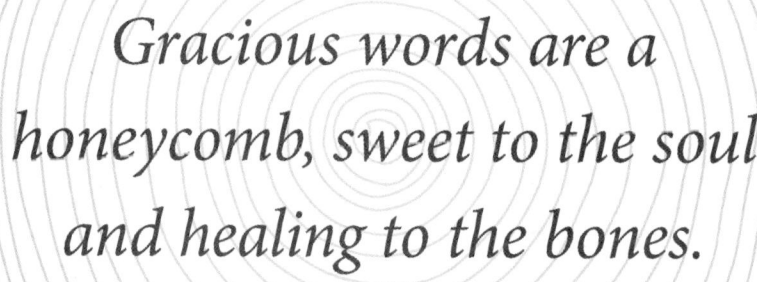

Gracious words are a honeycomb, sweet to the soul and healing to the bones.

Proverbs 16:24 NLT

I often think that the night is more alive and more richly colored than the day.

Vincent van Gogh

When things look dark

Just about every painting you see is of something in daylight. But there is something wonderful, even soothing, about the nocturne. Much of nature's creatures do their scavenging in the cool of the night while most of us are dreaming (of our next coloring page, of course).

To give you a little help, and save your pencils for another day, I went big time in adding the values to this moonlit scene. Coloring this scene is kind of like instant hot cocoa—just add water! Or in this case, just add color to transform this gray night to one of rich darks using your dark blues and purples to capture the serenity of the nighttime sky and ground below. Do you recognize the town? If not, look again at page 49.

To capture the luminescence of the moon, leave it pure white (the white of the paper) and then gently, gradually shade outwards from it using the circle or feathering shading technique (see Art Tip on page 80). Whatever color you choose for the glow, a warm yellow tone or a cool blue tone, that will be the color you should also use for the glow atop the clouds and land below, for it is the same light shining on all. Beethoven's *Moonlight Sonata* might be an apt choice to work by!

ACTION

"Rowing harder doesn't help if the boat is headed in the wrong direction." —Kenichi Ohmae

My ideal bedroom consists of a wall of east windows for the sun to greet me in the morning. I love getting up in the morning. It's a new day. A fresh start. "His mercies are new every morning…" I have tasted the brevity of life a few times and knowing that tomorrow is promised to no one, I see each day as a gift. No, I don't jump up and down with a party hat, but I have an anticipatory wonder of what's in store for the day.

I wasn't always like this. There was a time when I dreaded the day. I wondered what bad news would come my way.

I came across a book by David Lloyd-Jones some time ago that caused a paradigm shift in my thinking. Jones' essential message was that the will, not the emotion, should direct you. Doing the reverse results in a myriad of trouble and instability. I took note of the willful choices, challenges, admonitions, and commands throughout Scripture. They're everywhere. From "choose today whom you will serve" to "follow Me" to "rejoice". I put a "WA" for willful action beside each instance where a choice was involved, and next thing I knew, I began to see life as laden with opportunities. Opportunities to transform. "Be transformed by the renewing of your mind." (Romans 12:2 NIV).

I began to apply the concept of willful choices to my life, starting with my morning thoughts. A choice became a habit, shaping my vision, which gave my life purpose. I arise now and think "I'm awake, alive… already it's a good day." Mundane things become mini gifts and mini celebrations, from my first steps out of bed (thankful for a working body!) to seeing the weather (sun or rain, there is beauty to be had).

A friend and I kayak up the river together. It's a beautiful, tranquil experience, and as vigorous or easy as you desire. I quickly learned, however, that there is no such thing as sitting still in a river. If I don't row, the current carries me backwards, downstream. We only get to our destination by rowing.

Life is like that. By default, life's current flows opposite where we want to go. Bodies and things all break down over time. You have a choice: row towards your vision or coast away from it towards the fall. Yes, perseverance is soon at work here, too.

In the movie *The Family Man*, Téa Leoni's character, Kate, lived a life directed by one main resolve. "I choose us," she told her husband, Jack. She chose to focus on the love she had, rather than what she didn't have or what she forsook for that love. It was willful action that realized her vision for her life.

Ravi Zacharias shared a similar picture. "I remember the time an older man asked me when I was young, "Do you know what you are doing now?" I thought it was some kind of trick question. "Tell me," I said. "You are building your memories," he replied, "so make them good ones."

I have learned that either my will or my heart can chart my outlook, my vision, the course I will run. Is it not the shortsighted emotions that often throw us off course? The proverb "when the will is ready the feet are light" aptly states the difference our determination can make. Early in our marriage, my friend used to remind me that my heart would follow my will. What is your will, your desire? What will you aim and strive for? Simple, yes. Powerful, yes. Easy? Yes and no.

Something shady going on here

This is the same illustration from earlier in the book, but this time I have provided shading (also known as a value study). In the detail at right, colored pencil was added on top of the illustration above with very nice results. Remember to work with a light touch, gradually building up the values with multiple layers using crosshatching, circles, and other styles. Try using different colors in your mix, as well, such as using blues amidst your reds and browns. Notice the complements of violet and yellow playing off each other to enhance the candlelight effect!

I remember when I was younger and reading the Bible promise: "Take delight in the LORD, and he will give you the desires of your heart." I always focused on the second part, and began running off a list of desires that included a new car, new this, new that… I was delighting in everything but my Maker. I have since learned that if I delight in the one who loves me, then I end up being delighted. I have experienced the same thing with my relationships. When I sought the best for others, I found I was far more satisfied in that success than anything else. We oftentimes cannot change our circumstances, and we certainly cannot change what is past nor determine the future. But we can determine our response.

Join me in living a life of your choosing. One that is determined, focused, and purposeful.

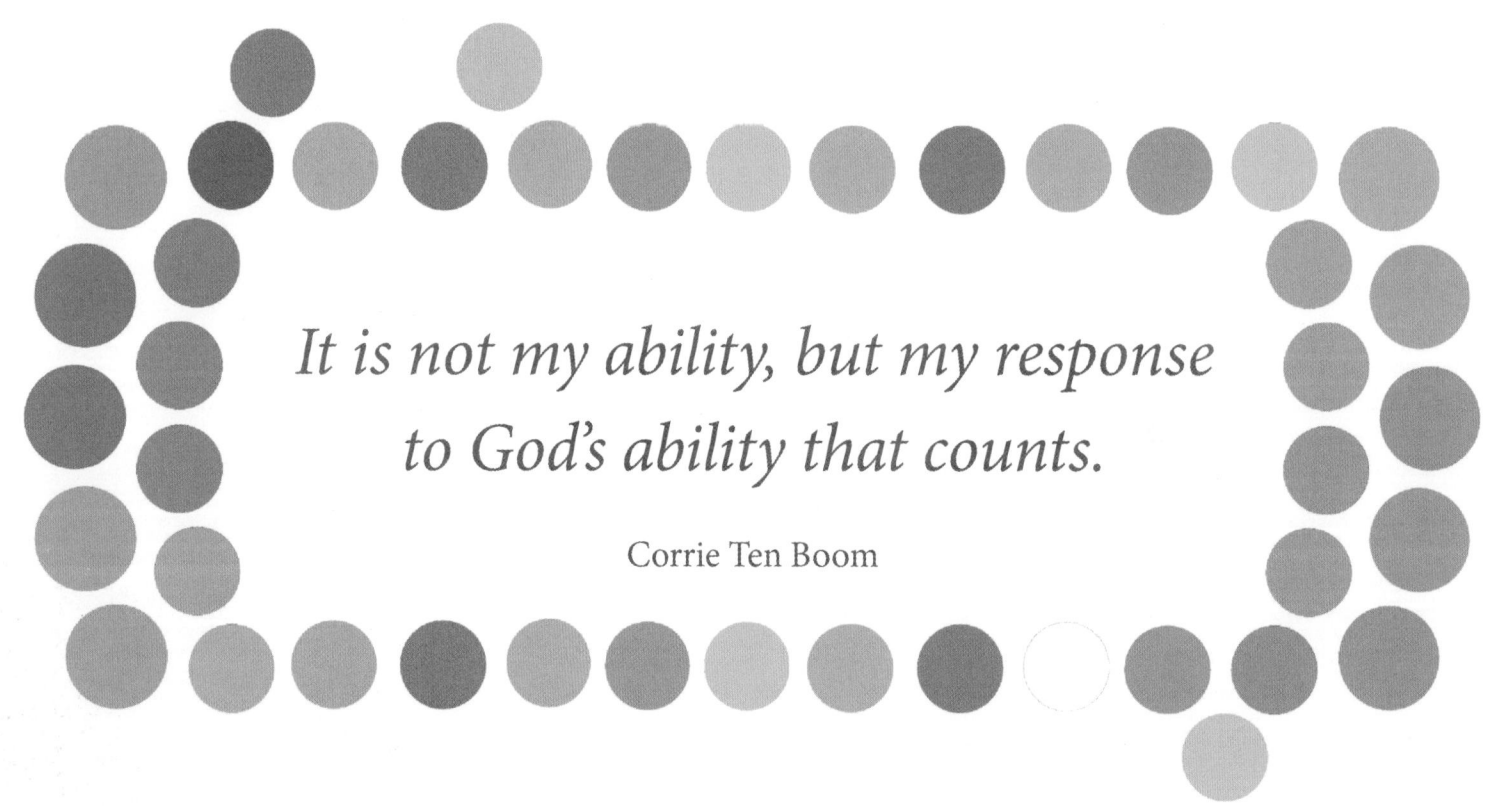

It is not my ability, but my response to God's ability that counts.

Corrie Ten Boom

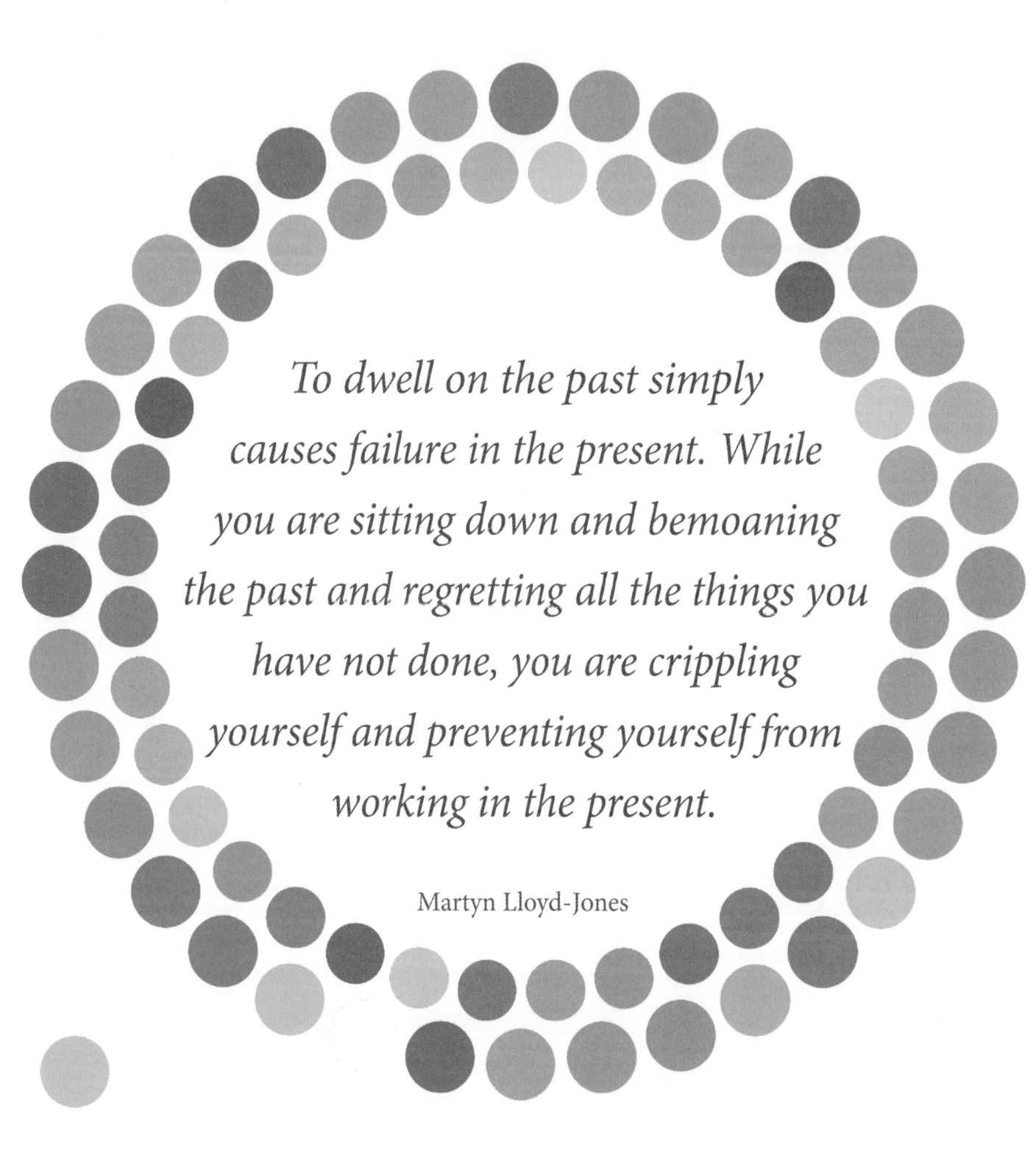

To dwell on the past simply causes failure in the present. While you are sitting down and bemoaning the past and regretting all the things you have not done, you are crippling yourself and preventing yourself from working in the present.

Martyn Lloyd-Jones

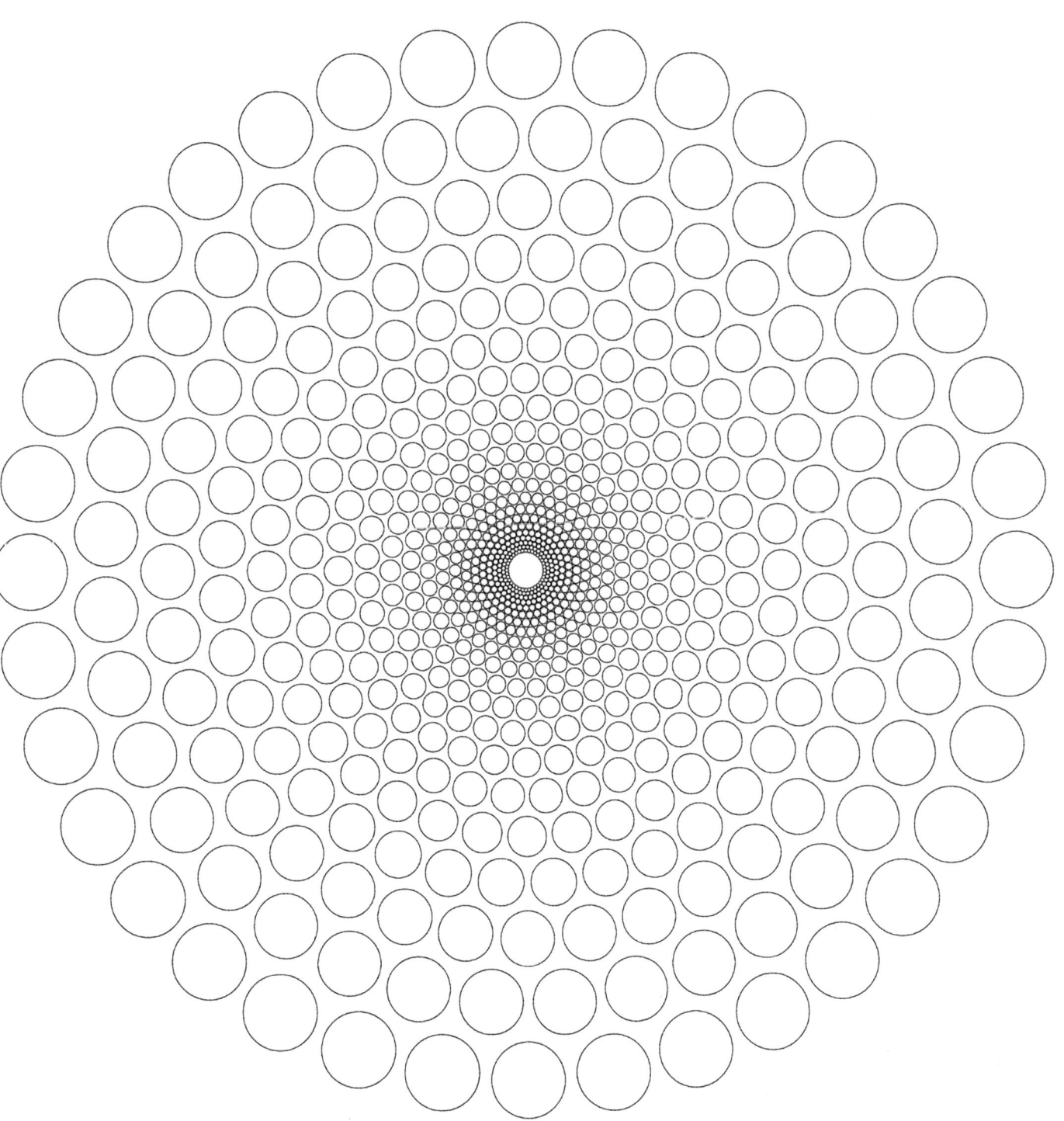

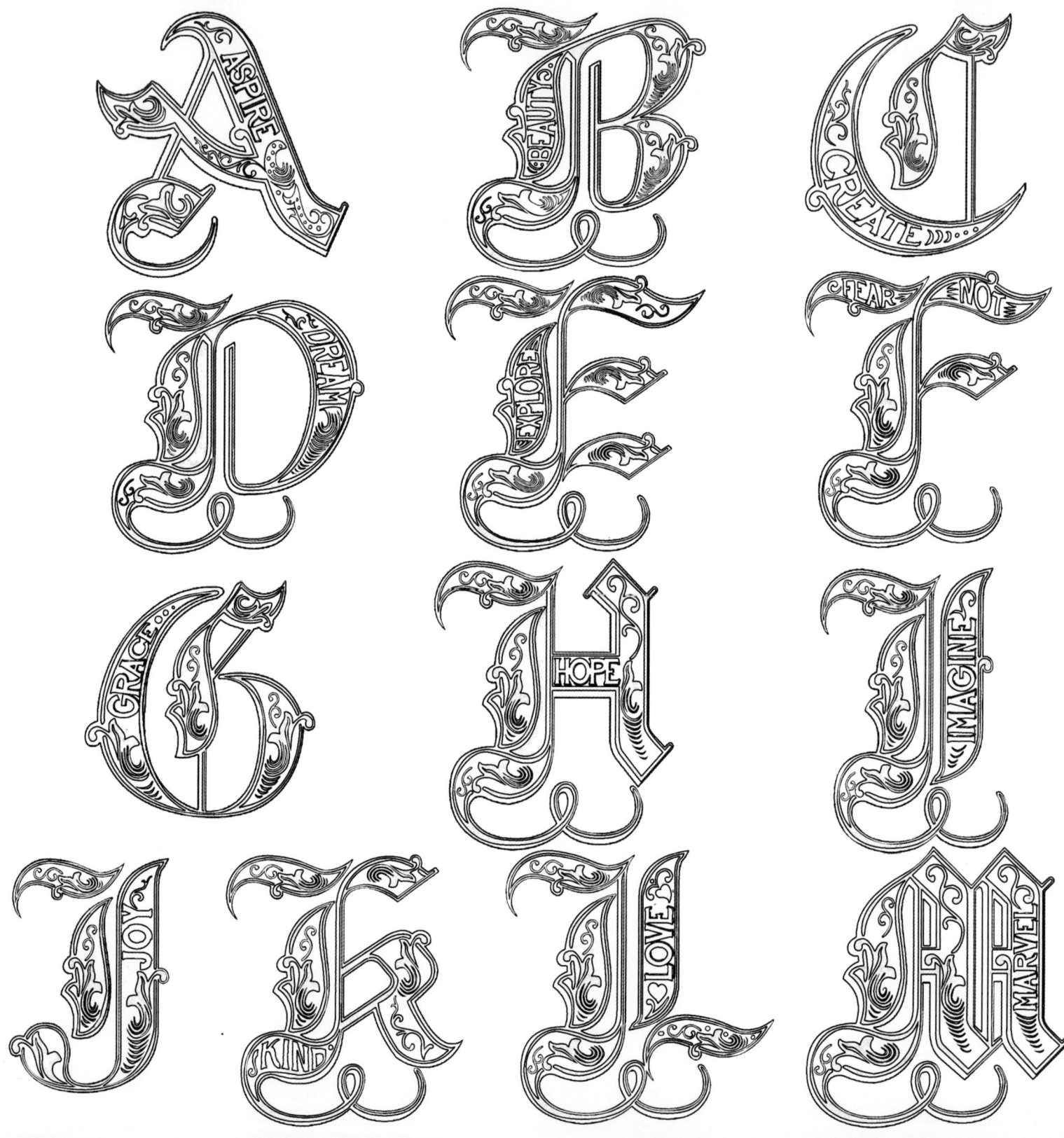

We have a right to believe whatever we want, but not everything we believe is right.

Ravi Zacharias

DESSERT

"A balanced diet is a cookie in each hand." —Barbara Johnson

Does the statement "A balanced diet is having a cookie or cupcake in each hand" make you smile? It does for me. I'm not even a cupcake aficionado, though Kim and I have a special date place in the city that makes nothing but amazing cupcakes. I appreciate dessert. Especially something with a good dark chocolate. Mmm mmm. Good last thoughts before I drift off to sleep at night.

They say you can't buy happiness, but you can buy dessert, and that's kind of the same thing. Another smile! We've talked about some great topics in this book—vision, perseverance, joy, action. All contribute to a life that is beautiful both for you and for others in your life. But where is the reward, here and in the hereafter? Reaching a goal, realizing a vision, persevering through a trial—they all deserve a celebration, which of course, should include dessert. Desserts, especially those with a candle aflame, say "celebration" as clearly as anything. Julia Child said, "A party without cake is just a meeting."

Celebrate! Celebrate everything: the day, the sunshine, your family, births and birthdays—every day. Celebrate love, dogs, meals, and other basic provisions. Celebrate the themes in this book—your dreams, opportunities, challenges (we grow from them), successes, benchmarks (steps towards your vision), and of course, crossing the finish line.

I think anyone would love being with someone who celebrates. Of course, with dessert, then it's a real celebration. I want my life to be a celebration. I also want it to be worthy of celebrating. My motto has become "I do because I can." Someday my body or circumstances may prevent me from doing something, but today, I am going to do whatever I can. It can be cleaning a mess for my bride, helping my kids, serving a stranger. It could be hard labor (I love a body that works, especially a body tired from work), or whatever comes my way that day.

But then I want to celebrate the day, the moment, the effort. I can celebrate with a cool glass of iced tea on the porch, a warm cup of hot cocoa by the fire, or best yet…something chocolate…anywhere!

There's another celebration at the real true end of this life that I am really looking forward to. Jesus said, "The kingdom of heaven is like a king who prepared a wedding banquet for his son" (Matthew 22:2 NIV). You know weddings have the best desserts! However, from what I understand, heaven is dessert compared to life on this side of eternity.

That is one celebration I am definitely looking forward to. It's also worth envisioning, persevering for, and enjoying imagining until I get there. We are all invited, though not everyone accepts the invitation (you'll have to read the story yourself in Matthew 22). I didn't do anything to get invited, and there were no conditions, rules, or dress code. We're simply invited to join our Maker, to celebrate his son, Jesus.

Like my kids who bubble with anticipation of an upcoming vacation, an eternity free of the thorns and toil and tears of this life is worth getting excited about. In short, it's worth persevering through the changes, imagining the vision, enjoying the trip there. I look forward to celebrating with you, assuming you'll be attending? Hope so! The dessert will top them all, your heart's desire.

Life is short.

Eat dessert first.

Crisp and clean for shiny syrup!

To obtain a shiny surface, such as on the syrup topping on the ice cream, keep your edges crisp and clean rather than soft and fuzzy. Think of liquid like chrome, glass, or ceramic. Reflections have crisp, hard edges to them, and surfaces are slick with no texture. Your syrup should be a definite contrast to the ice cream, which has a texture, and is dull rather than shiny.

I couldn't resist turning this illustration into my favorite combination ice cream dish: chocolate mint chip with hot fudge and whipped cream on top! Notice that I barely did any shading to the whipped cream, and honestly, I was too hungry to finish coloring the bowl. You can color your syrup to be strawberry or caramel to go with your favorite ice cream. Or invent a new flavor!

Scatter joy.

Ralph Waldo Emerson

Art Tip

Bookmarks and note cards

Enjoy coloring these bookmarks and note cards. Cut along the borders, then laminate your creations for a long-lasting keepsake or gift.

Cut bookmarks and note cards along border on the other side.

Life is good.

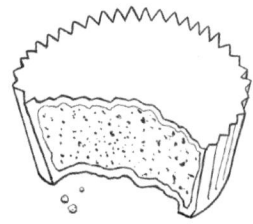

Bert and John Jacobs

17°—TIM'S STORY

Did you know that a hawk's range of vision spans approximately 290 degrees? Talk about seeing things. No wonder a field mouse has no chance when a hawk is watching. A hawk sees a whopping 60 percent more than you (human have a visual field of 180 degrees)! Dogs and cats have 240 degrees, about 40 percent more range than us two-leggers.

Among people, artists are blessed with better vision, musicians with better hearing, right? Actually, no. Beethoven was deaf, Monet had cataracts. My visual range is a tad less than yours by about 160 degrees, coming in at 17 degrees. In other words, about 10 percent of yours. In fact, the government considers me legally blind since my range is below their minimum threshold of 20 degrees.

The funny thing? I earn my livelihood as a professional portrait artist, which my dad calls the king of art genres due to its difficulty. And people wonder if God has a sense of humor? A guy with less than 10 percent of normal vision earning his living doing something as precise and challenging as painting portraits. Crazy.

I am Tim Chambers, professional artist and founder of Iguana Art Academy. I've been painting professionally for twenty-five years, and have been around art my whole life since my dad, William Chambers, is also a professional artist (WilliamChambers.com). I probably made my career choice by the time I was three. I love art. I can't imagine being anything else. It's how I see the world. The created world, people, relationships, philosophy, purpose—everything. I see moments as paintings.

People have asked me how I can paint when I see so little. Actually, I see much more than most people see. I lack peripheral vision, true, but I can see what I am looking at, and for an artist, that's what truly matters. Even better is an artist who can see the beauty in the commonplace. "Anything under the sun is beautiful if you have the vision; it is the seeing of the thing that makes it so," taught American painter Charles Hawthorne. I agree.

Growing up, I always knew I was going to be an artist. However, I could never have guessed the journey that awaited me. "Even the best-laid plans of mice and men go awry," said poet Robert Burns. Still, when I convinced my dad that my resolve matched my artistic gifts, I began training to make art a profession. After all, I would be competing with Dad, and I had much to learn.

College was an adventure, but not the kind I expected. My dad had set a high standard. I studied at a time when abstract, psychological-based art was the norm. Even the best colleges were about conveying feeling, not what we see. The only absolute was that there were no absolutes, and certainly no clear definitions of what constituted beauty. Always one to find a solution, my dad discovered a school down in Nashville, Tennessee, that taught traditional tools of illustration—anatomy, composition, lettering, and more. I would be transferring from a school of 25,000 students to one of ninety. Yes, ninety. The Harris School of Art in Franklin, Tennessee, had less than 1 percent the students from my college. Did someone say small?

I was enjoying my first semester at Harris, learning southern-speak ("Coke" referred to all soft drinks, not just one, and some one-syllable words were now two) when my dad called and said he found a school that might interest me: Atelier Lack, in balmy Minneapolis, Minnesota. It was Richard Lack's atelier (French for studio), and he accommodated a maximum of twelve apprentices. 25,000 to 90 to 12. Smaller...a clue of things to come. I said goodbye to my friends at Harris and trekked up to Minneapolis after Christmas. Studying at Atelier Lack was a great experience, as I learned centuries-old practices of drawing and painting. It was classic. Literally. I was surrounded by very serious students who lived and breathed traditional painting. Patience was a virtue I learned here, as we would work on one drawing for over a month. Heretofore I had worked no more than a day on a drawing. Steady and meticulous was the way of life here.

I enjoyed studying under Mr. Lack. He was an amazing painter with a wry wit. Stephen Gjertson was my other instructor there. Both were patient, kind, serious painters and teachers, generous and enthusiastic to share what they knew with us younger painters. I learned the art of seeing at Atelier Lack. I also made some good friends. One of my favorite friends, one of the few who can handle (and exceed) my wacky sense of humor, is Carl Samson. Carl is an outright incredible artist. I think between Carl and me, we transformed Atelier Lack from a deathly serious school to one alive with humor.

While studying at Lack's, my dad found out about an American master teaching in Provincetown, Massachusetts. The Cape School of Art was started a hundred years earlier by American master Charles Hawthorne, a student of another master, William Merritt Chase. Artists who studied here include Emile Gruppe, Norman Rockwell, Max Bohm and Richard Miller. The current teacher carrying on the tradition was 84-year-old American Impressionist Henry Hensche, a student of Hawthorne. My best friend, Kevin, and I drove out to the Cape in my '74 Firebird (a beauty with a great stereo). Studying at Ptown would change how I see the world and strike a chord in my heart that resonates stronger than ever today, thirty years later.

Cloudy Day Block Study by Timothy J. Chambers

Prior to meeting Henry Hensche, my focus had been on accurate drawing. I had honed my drawing skills, developing my sense of values (shading) and draftsmanship, trusting my dad's counsel: "Color will come; first excel at drawing, Tim." In fact, I was so focused on that goal that I had not given any attention to studying any of the great painters of the past. In one simple exchange, Henry Hensche revealed my dirth of awareness and opened up a golden opportunity. Here's the gist of that conversation:

SCENE: Kevin and I painting in what was called the "Sand Pit" behind the Cape School—a small yard consisting of tall, gray wood tables, weathered by decades of salt, cold winter winds, and hot summer sun. We were painting colored blocks—the standard training tool of the Cape School. I was struggling with capturing the colors of a yellow block. When I mixed black and yellow to paint the shady side of the block, my yellow turned green. Ugh. I was clueless. Along comes Henry to check in and see how I am doing.

HENRY HENSCHE: How is it going? What's your name? Where are you from?
TIM: Hi, Mr. Hensche. I'm Tim, and this is Kevin. We're from Chicago.
HENRY: How long have you been painting?
TIM: About an hour, maybe.
HENRY: No, I meant forever. How long have you been painting in your life? Beginners?
TIM: Never. I mean, first time, really. Yes, beginners.
HENRY: Have you seen Monet?

TIM: Who? (I didn't know any better, but I should have been embarrassed, being at a school studying Impressionism and I didn't even know who the founder of Impressionism was.)

HENRY: Monet. Claude Monet. Never mind. Having trouble with that yellow block, eh? Let me have your palette and brush. You can get rid of that tube of burnt umber, and the black too.

I watched as Henry drew from my piles of violet, blue, red, and white, to paint the most stunning, beautiful, true yellow block I've ever seen. He barely even used any yellow. I was stunned. I was hooked. As Henry handed me my palette, he said "This weekend, you two go to the Gardner in Boston and look at the Monets. M-O-N-E-T. Monet."

Kevin and I took the ferry to Boston to visit the Gardner Museum and see the Monets. At first glance, up close, I wasn't impressed. I moved on. Kevin stayed at the first painting, one of Monet's Haystack paintings. From across the room I looked back for Kevin and suddenly, I was stunned. Again. Two stunning moments in a week. The Monet was the most amazing painting I had ever seen. The colors were life-like, full of sun, full of air, full of…reality. My life would never be the same. Kevin saw it before me, up close. It took me stepping away to see how everything pulled together.

Meadow with Poplars by Claude Monet 1875

We went back to the Cape School with a new awareness, convinced we were in the most perfect place in the world. Once, during a talk and demonstration, Henry challenged the students to "be like those two innocent boys (Kevin and me) from Chicago. They don't know anything!" (We were initially very insulted, but we learned Henry was actually encouraging students to lay aside their preconceived notions and see with fresh eyes.) Henry would open our eyes that week to see what we had missed all along. To see what most people don't see. Color. Real color. And he would begin to teach us how to respond to what we were observing. Everything was new. Even ordinary things were now amazing.

It was there that I met the man who would become my most influential teacher outside of my dad: Cedric Egeli. Cedric invited me to come down to Annapolis to study with him. After one more semester in Minneapolis, I did. Cedric, already one of the best portrait artists in America, was studying color with Henry. Cedric was like my dad, always humble, searching for a way to improve. Between those two men, I have learned to be satisfied only in seeking, observing, examining, and growing. Cedric and his wife, Joanette, also an amazing painter who captures the heart like few can, invited me into their home to study painting and color. 25,000 to 90 to 12 to 1. Little did I see the Gideon-like reduction in numbers, the narrowing of my path.

I studied with the Egelis and Henry Hensche for a while after that, even after I entered into the professional portrait painting field. Again, while I was chomping at the bit to turn professional, my teachers advised me to learn and study as long as I could. Wise counsel. I thank God and my parents for the privilege to do just that.

While I honed my mind and skills to be an artist, my heart was also demanding growth. There were questions that had nothing to do with shapes and values and line and form. Questions about my identity apart from art, questions that hung like a candle with no candle holder. Wax was dripping, and my heart was demanding an answer.

One of my high school buddies, Bob, had a beautiful younger sister. I had always enjoyed flirting with girls, but Kim was off-limits to his buddies, per Bob's orders. But one time at Bob's house, I noticed Kim reading. I went to say hi (and yes, flirt). Kim was a sight, but it was her book, a Bible, that garnered my attention. Not sure why. I had never read a Bible. But curious I was. I convinced her brother to let Kim join us guys as we headed out for midnight milkshakes, and it was there that Kim gave insight to some of the questions that had been brewing. I didn't get a date, but I did get a book. And some answers.

Fast forward two years. I had been reading that book for a couple years before it all came together for me. My appetite for truth in art carried over to life as well. My parents taught me to embrace knowledge and learning. Logic was kind of a game of wits in our house. I was intrigued by the idea of exploring this God thing.

If God was real, if he was true, then I wanted to know him. Funny thing was that a book that was always near (I grew up going to church) but never opened, now had the answers my heart and mind were seeking. That winter, at Christmas time, I began to center my view of life on Christ. Like the story of the apostle Peter in John 6:68, I couldn't find any other way or philosophy that would satisfy the deepest longings in my heart and mind. I now had two purposes: to know God, and to be a painter. I was curious how the two would meet.

Fast forward again, another six years. After about ten years of studying art, I married the forbidden Kim (with her brother's blessing) and we moved to Maryland where I began life as a professional artist. My career took off quickly. I received many commissions, raising my fees rapidly to stem the demand. I won major awards for my work. I was doing well, and I envisioned it wouldn't be long until I was painting presidents, my portraits hanging alongside other great paintings in Washington. The future was bright.

I know what you're thinking. Those are dangerous words. The older and wiser know that life sometimes has a way of tempering our lofty ambitions, of bringing our dreams down to the unforgiving reality of life on earth. So it was with me.

When I was thirty, on the heels of coming in second place for my portrait *Ashley* in an international portrait competition (my friend Carl Samson, whom I had convinced to enter the contest, won first prize), I went in for my annual routine eye checkup. It started fine, but routine quickly turned to horror when the doctor's face went from relaxed to concerned. "Something's not right. You need to see a retinal specialist." The feeling was dread, it was silence, it was fear, it was unfamiliar, it couldn't be. Please, no.

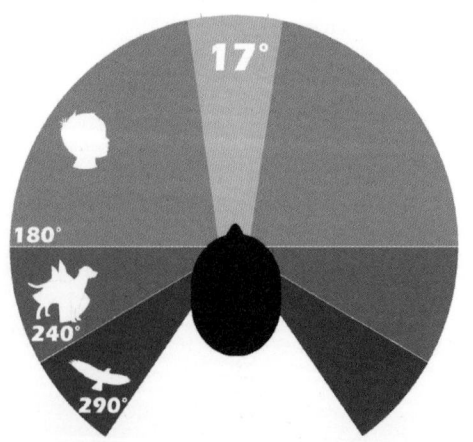

Kim and I were referred to a retinal specialist near Washington, D.C. My worst fears were confirmed. I had Usher Syndrome, a degenerative disease in which one steadily loses their hearing and vision. Unfortunately, my specialist lacked any sense of bedside manners. In an effort to provide some background as we considered a plan of action, I brought a portfolio of my award-winning portraits for him to view. He flipped through a few pages then thrust it back into my hands, and with the warmth of a surgical knife, said "Better find another profession." Ugh. Oh, that hurt. To this day, I cringe when that tape plays in my mind.

My life suddenly lost its footing. My future? Not so bright. In fact, I was convinced, per Dr. Retinal Specialist, that it was stark, midnight black. I was an artist. I saw the world in living color. In a blink my identity was shaken. Gone.

Or so I thought. Kim—I can't thank God enough for her—was with me every step. Though I thought my life was over, Kim assured me it wasn't. A friend and pastor assured me that though I may be surprised, my Maker wasn't. All but three people said, "Oh, God would never take your sight, since he's gifted you as an artist." No, anyone knows that you don't dictate to a sovereign God what he can and cannot do. He even tells Darth Vader, the ocean, and the universe where their limits end. God can and does do whatever he pleases. Kim reminded me that life was more than painting, and that I was more than a painter. I met that with fear. My pastor and friend Larry said that creativity was part of who I was, and nothing could squelch it. It would come out one way or another.

A few people offered reassurance with the oft-quoted verse, "'I know the plans I have for you,' declares the Lord, 'plans to prosper you and not to harm you, plans to give you hope and a future'" (Jeremiah 29:11 NIV).

We've heard this promise many times, and we post it on our walls, even stating it like a mantra, trusting that good things are on their way to our doorstep. After the news I had just received, I thought truly I must be the exception to this promise. My future looked the opposite of what this verse promises.

However, sadly, no one ever quotes Jeremiah 29:10, the verse immediately preceding 29:11. Claiming the promise of verse 11 without considering the context leads to dismay and wondering why God doesn't keep his promises. Jeremiah 29:10 says, "This is what the Lord says: 'When seventy years are completed for Babylon, I will come to you and fulfill my good promise to bring you back to this place.'" A few verses earlier we read that it was God who carried the Israelites away from their home via a Babylonian siege. Pack a suitcase and get out. No chance of selling their homes to net some equity, transfer their IRAs or 401Ks, empty their house with a yard sale or Craigslist. No, they lost everything.

It was upon such circumstances that God yields the promise of hope and a future, safe in the love and protection and provision of their Creator. Not the kind of promise that would sell well, even with today's savvy marketing. I wondered what was in store. What and who could I count on?

Joshua & Kayla by Timothy J. Chambers

It took me a couple years to learn to deal with the news of my eye/ear disease. My worst fear was that I would lose my sight and hearing completely and be relegated to a rocking chair in the living room, waiting for someone to come and touch me and say hello. I feared that my life would become nothing, that I would have nothing to offer. I feared that I would be forgotten, dismissed, losing all dignity—a mere inconvenience in the lives of those who could still live fully. It was a deep fear, and it would take time for me to release it and trust that God truly does have plans for a hope and a future for me even if I was exiled from what I thought was good and normal.

The original diagnosis ("find another profession") played mercilessly in my head, paralyzing me at times. In fact, I didn't get a full night of sleep for almost two years due to waking up in a cold sweat, fearful of what lay ahead. It was our family physician who told me that the health fears taunting me resided in my imagination. He said "Tim, this is an issue of faith and trust. You're healthy. Go live."

It wasn't until I began to take my physician's advice and begin to trust that God is greater than everything, including my disease and all my fears, that I began to move past the fear. Either God is or is not. Or he does not exist. There is no other option. I recall sharing the original physician's diagnosis with Dr. Irene Maumenee, then head of Wilmar Eye Institute at Johns Hopkins Hospital, one of the leading eye centers in the world. Her response? "Find another profession? No! Tim, you paint until you can't!" Even now, as I write her charge, I get shivers of joy and thankfulness. Yes, that is how we should live, echoing Jonathan Swift's wisdom: "May you live all the days of your life."

Jackson by Timothy J. Chambers

I left there with a new lease on life. Instead of living in dread, I began to live with opportunity again. Though fear may be a part of the battle, we need to prevail. Boxer Muhammad Ali once said impossible is an opinion. I add that impossible is an opportunity. You'll meet naysayers anywhere you turn. You can lay down and die, or you can live.

A good portrait painting is 50 percent a matter of an understanding, empathetic, insightful heart; 50 percent observation, and 20 percent execution. I was never great at math, but I insist this is true. Many people can copy, and many can see, but few understand with their mind and heart. I face fears face-to-face and overcome them because I simply have to as much as I have to breath. My heart tells me that God is greater, and he promises I can enjoy peace in the future if I trust him with the now.

On a lighter note, the declining vision has its humorous side. You've got your 200 degrees of peripheral side-to-side vision, and I've got my 17 degrees. You'd win at basketball, of course. But I can see what I'm looking at. Yes, my dog runs when she sees me coming, and I get dirty looks from accidentally bumping and poking people or cutting in line unaware, but it can be funny. I'll give you an example.

My kids and I were shopping for a Christmas present for Kim. We came upon a display of electronic massaging products, which we thought Kim would like due to her chronic stiff neck and shoulder from an auto accident (drugged driver). My youngest daughter immediately tried out the massage chair on my left, and my son, standing next to me on my right, and I looked over the various packages for an ideal gift. While I was reading one box, I was unaware that my son had moved to the opposite side of the display. I casually picked up a box to my right, and suddenly I was in a tug-of-war with my son over the box. I jokingly said, "Would you just let go of it already?!" Only it wasn't my son. I glanced to my right, but he's wasn't there. My daughter was still in the chair. Gasp! I saw my son standing six feet away from me, mortified, shaking his head *No, Dad, no*. I thought, *If he's there, and Chloe's to my left, who's on the other end of this box?* I looked up to find an elderly woman scowling at me, determined to have this box. I gave up the battle, smiled, and said, "Oh, hey, Merry Christmas!" I turned away, embarrassed (a little bit), smiling, laughing. Another memory video clip for my kids.

That's just one of many. I am convinced God has a great sense of humor. I'm an entertainment factory. October 2013 marked twenty years since I was diagnosed with Usher. I am glad that I didn't take the advice of the initial retinal specialist. Imagine if I had stopped painting twenty years ago. What a waste of life and joy and happiness and talent that would have been, akin to burying it in the sand. Instead, I continue to paint. And to my delight, I continue to improve, having recently delivered what I feel is my best portrait yet.

Is it hard? Yes, it gets more challenging as time goes on. I believe that our troubles are not about the person afflicted, but about those around him or her. My family adjusts to accommodate me—repeating things several times, making sure nothing is left out of place (TRIP), or open (BAM, OW!), or alerting me if they walk away (*Hello?* and embarrassment as I assumed they're next to me and I'm talking to…no one). Living with a disability has certainly made me sensitive, aware, and sympathetic to others that suffer.

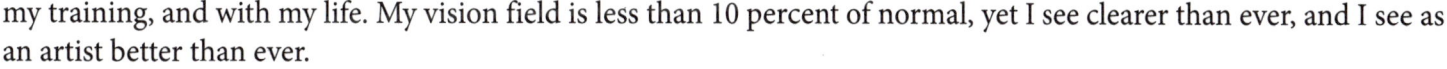

It's also given me a chance to trust God more and more. I have to, really. But who am I? With the little vision I have left, who am I to be painting portraits? I'm not supposed to be able to do what I do. Even eye doctors have asked, "How do you manage to do what you do?!" Yet, I do. And yes, I do have to deal with the reality that I don't know what lies ahead for me. But then again, so do you.

25,000 to 90 to 12 to 1. God seems to work in terms of reduction, doesn't he? He did so with Gideon, with sending Jesus to fulfill the role as Savior (the odds of 350+ prophesies fulfilled in one person? Crazy!). He did it with me in regards to my training, and with my life. My vision field is less than 10 percent of normal, yet I see clearer than ever, and I see as an artist better than ever.

I have learned, as have many others, that life isn't always about Jeremiah 29:11. If you think it's about having a warm, cozy, successful life, watch out. Don't get cynical, hopeless, careless, or fearful. Look at history, human nature, and the heart. There is something much more grand than me and my moment. It's not about getting, but responding. Jeremiah 29:10 tells us that there is a different timetable than the one with which we measure time. God's timetable is very long term. As in eternally long term. This life isn't about seizing my glory, but about seeing the tapestry being woven throughout many lifetimes. It's a beautiful tapestry, made up of threads bright (happy times), dark (hard times), and grays (stay-the-course times). As any painter knows, you need all three types to create a beautiful work.

My best painting may actually not be painted with oil, but with joy. I'm starting to see that a smile can do wonders. I'm finding that creativity itself is a beautiful thing. It can breed smiles, joy, and these make the world—yours and mine—a better place for everyone. That's my desire for you and the people I meet.

Thanks for hearing my story. What's yours? I'd love to hear it.

IGUANA ART ACADEMY

iguanaacademy.com

Iguana Art Academy is where you have fun developing creativity, skills, and confidence—in a vibrant community of creatives! Discover a variety of courses with awesome instruction and personal feedback, accessed anytime, anywhere. We are happiness 24/7.

ANYTIME, ANYWHERE

Iguana is ready whenever and wherever you are, 24/7, on all devices.

HELLO, FRIENDS

Iguana is a thriving community to hang and talk shop with friends!

"GOOD JOB!"

Enjoy personal feedback and encouragement from peers and instructors.

With the purchase of this book, you get the online instructional coloring course "Color Beautiful" at Iguana Art Academy for free. Iguana offers a variety of interactive courses that are engaging and make learning fun! The Color Beautiful art course gives in-depth demonstrations of the book's illustrations and art tips to expand your creative skills.

Enroll in your free Color Beautiful course at IguanaAcademy.com/courses

Enter coupon code *COLOR-BEAUTIFUL-FREE* at checkout to begin your course

In addition to the fun at Iguana Art Academy, join the excitement of *Seeing Beautiful* at SeeingBeautiful.com and at Facebook.com/SeeingBeautiful